From the Abyss

John Emil Augustine

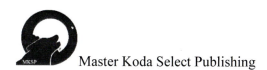

Master Koda Select Publishing

From the Abyss

An MKSP Book/July 2014

Published by Master Koda Select Publishing, LLC
www.masterkodaselectpublishing.com

Text copyright © 2013 John Emil Augustine

All rights reserved

The right of John Emil Augustine to be identified as the author of this work has been asserted by him in accordance with the Copyright, Designs and Patents Act 1988.

Originally published in eBook form by Master Koda Select Publishing in 2013

Master Koda Select Publishing, LLC functions only as the book publisher and as such, the ultimate design, content, editorial accuracy, and views expressed or implied in this work are those of the author.

No part of this publication may be reproduced, stored in a retrieval system, or transmitted in any way by any means without the prior permission of the copyright holder, except as provided by USA copyright law.

ISBN-10: 0990587819
ISBN-13: 978-0-9905878-1-1

Cover Art Design © Rebbekah White
Stock footage provided by Kamira/Pond5.com

Dedication

I dedicate this work to those who are living (or who have ever lived) with abuse. My hope is that stories such as this will provide you with a glimpse of your own inner beauty and right to freedom. Hope and help will come. Watch for it, and in the meantime, believe in your value and protect yourself. Reach out to those who offer sanctuary.

Thank you

I need a mess of help to stand alone, so thank you with all my heart to Brenda Perlin, Judy L. Brekke, Lynelle Clark, Richard Novy, Fran Lewis, Marsha Casper-Cook, Kim Mutch Emerson, Sarah L. Wallace, White Buffalo Calf Woman, Holiness David Running Eagle, Ishtar Babilu Dingir, Olivia, and most importantly, to my greatest teacher and best friend, my wife.

From the Abyss   John Emil Augustine

Table of Contents

So Long, John 1

The Sign 5

Set Up 12

A Good Start 19

The Deal Breaker...Or Not 21

The Real Deal-Breaker 23

Surprise 31

The Slow Drag 35

Happiness Hidden 43

Time to Transition 49

For Worse 54

Perhaps Answers 62

Crazy 67

Escape 72

Recapture 77

Familiar Voice 79

Total Eclipse 84

One Ticket to Paradise 91

Coming Clean 95

The Opposite Decision 100

Someplace Fun 108

Losing the Battle 114

An Ending and a Beginning 124

CD Release Party 132

Away from the Edge 136

From the Abyss   John Emil Augustine

Crap in Paradise 142

One More Time 155

A New Year 159

A Weird Turn 163

Don't Look Back 167

Heart Hardened 171

Spring Backward 174

Knock Outs and Knock Offs 185

Aimlessness 190

Hitting Bottom 193

The Beautiful Moon 201

Love Seen From Hell 210

Foreword

What first prompted me to start writing this was my friend whom I have always thought of as my kid sister. She had recently gone through a tough relationship, and I wanted to do something to help. She was living away from home and was trying to process her own episode while dealing with homesickness. I thought by giving her my story in small installments, about a chapter a day, she would have something to look forward to each day and to which she could possibly relate. Had it not been for her encouragement throughout the process, this book would not have been written. She seemed to like the story enough to encourage me to keep writing as I went, rough as my writing was in its rushed state.

An excellent writer in her own right and of a far more literary background than I, her admiration and thoughtful reactions as the story progressed were what kept me at it. I typed it up in the warehouse where I work, on breaks and in the few quiet moments between shipping and receiving, then sent it to her each day at the end of my shift. It was interesting that when my mind was already on the topic, doing the manual labor gave me a chance to arrange my thoughts before I sat down to write. I ended up working on my warehouse tasks specifically because I needed time to process what I was going to write next...oh, and because that's what I'm paid to do, though the pay was admittedly secondary during that time. I came to realize that neither act, the manual nor the intellectual labor, was much different than the other. They both were harmonious, simultaneous actions. One gave my mind a break, and the other, my body a break. In so doing, I never got tired of my work, the warehouse nor the writing. How strangely complimentary, though seemingly unrelated, some things can be!

While I was learning about my own writing process, I figured I was helping my friend too. I think what I wrote did help in a small way, but by the end, she wasn't receptive to my conclusions. Nor would I have been in her shoes. She was not ready to move on, and I completely understood. We did not end up seeing eye to eye, but we were able to discuss our difference of opinion. That discussion was most important to both of us.

Everyone views the same thing in a different way, and the importance of storytelling has a lot to do with the ensuing discussion. We need such discussions as a larger community to collectively better ourselves as inhabitants of the planet. Our stories can serve multiple purposes, and thus far this one has served one. Perhaps it will serve a purpose for you as well. Please feel free to let me know if it does. As I once did with the stories I used to tell in my own English classes, I certainly welcome discussion.

Enjoy the story. It is true, and it is here almost exactly as I sent it to my friend, my kid sister, from late March to early May 2012 in chapter installments.

John Emil Augustine, July 2012

So Long, John

The hot, humid Minneapolis summer was cooling, and the city streets no longer waved heat as they had just a few short weeks before. Landscaping had been tough that summer. I remember being told to sit down and drink water one squelching August afternoon as my mind went a little hazy from working so hard in the hundred degree heat. Landscaping could be a tough gig.

Now, by early September, the powerful sun was waning, and the concrete behind the landscaping office was finally cooling. I sat on my lunch break with Emily. Everyone else was on assignment, so she asked me to join her for lunch that day. Her tousled red curls waved in the wind and glistened in the sunlight. Her faded freckles, though accompanied by laugh lines and faint wrinkles, still gave her face a youthful look. I loved to hear her laugh and to hear her up-beat, confident, sweet voice. To be in her presence at the age of 25, even though she was 37, was incredibly thrilling.

She was married. I was getting married. I didn't care. I didn't want to sleep with her – not really. We had too little in common for me to really entertain that notion. The idea of Emily as a conquest or an ideal lovemaking partner had certainly gone through my mind, but something had never been right about those thoughts. I understand the un-guyness of such a statement, but there it is.

Torrid sexual tension wasn't actually what made the relationship interesting. This was a better relationship than that. Better than sex. This was my little taste of heaven. This was my reminder of what I was looking for, what I had been looking for until I decided to get married. In fact, my fiancé, Cindi, and I had actually been set up by Emily. I was following Emily's recommendation. The way I looked at it, I was marrying the next-best thing to Emily.

At the worn, wooden picnic table behind the office, Emily ate her hummus and veggies, and I sat with my peanut butter sandwich and chips, looking at her and then at the trees behind her. They were beginning, just a little, to turn. Everything I had experienced that summer, especially my courtship with Cindi, was changing and most certainly cooling. Cindi was changing. Emily knew. She understood me like a best friend. She sensed my apprehension and had seen Cindi change first-hand. She knew my predicament well.

"John?" Her head tilted.

I looked at her and saw the concern on her beautiful face. I knew what we were going to talk about. I knew she felt as if she should at least broach the subject. She had always looked out for me.

"Yeah," I said nonchalantly.

"Are you doing ok?"

"Yeah, I'm fine."

"You know Cindi's not talking to me, right?"

"Yeah, it's childish. I know."

"Well, that's between me and her, but I am worried about you. If you ever need help, just let me know, and I will try to help you."

"I know…I think I will be ok."

"I really don't want to put her down, but I know she can be difficult sometimes."

"No, you're right. I can see that pretty objectively. She was awful to you, and I can't apologize for her, but…"

"John, no. Don't apologize."

"I know, but I want you to know it isn't your fault. That's how she is. She's mean to people for no reason."

"John, I have to ask…are you sure about this?"

"About what? The wedding?"

"I don't want to talk you out of it; I just want to know that you're walking into this with your eyes open."

"Here's what I think. Cindi needs…help. She needs someone to care for her and to be a voice of reason." I was surprised at myself when I heard my own words. What was I getting myself into?

"She does. I agree." Emily sighed.

She must have known something about what I was getting myself into, I realized. Then, because I realized her awareness of the tottering perch upon which I was balanced, I suddenly felt the need to convince her that I was doing the right thing, that I had the situation under control.

"She trusts me, Emily. So long as she trusts me, I can be that person for her. She knows she gets out of line. She just doesn't know when it's called for and when it's not. She needs someone who will help with that. I think I can do it."

"I just wish you could wait. Your wedding is next month. Can't you wait till spring?"

"Of course we could wait. Of course."

I looked away, trailing off. How beautiful the trees would look in a few weeks. By the time the wedding happened, the leaves would be brown and mostly fallen. But between now and then, I could enjoy this one last reprieve, this beautiful change from green to brilliant red, orange, and yellow. I could enjoy my freedom one last time. And I could enjoy my moment with Emily.

"Then why don't you?"

I broke from my thoughts as a wave of anger went through me, and all my frustration suddenly boiled to the surface as I snapped, "You don't get it, Emily!"

"John!" Her face flashed shock. She had never seen me like that. I had rarely seen myself like that.

"Sorry. I'm so sorry." I immediately put my head down in shame, suddenly shaking.

"John, you're not ok. Please let me help somehow. This isn't you."

"I know. I'm just tired, that's all. I'm so sorry. I don't know what came over me."

"I'm worried about you, John. Do you have my number?"

"No."

"Here, I'll write it down for you, just in case. I don't care why you call; just tell me you'll call if you need anything. If you need a place to sleep for the night, someone to vent to, whatever. Just tell me you'll call."

I nodded my head obediently. "Ok, I'll call."

"Here. Put this somewhere safe."

"Ok. Thank you."

"All right, Duke, I better get back in there," she said, pulling herself away from me and the conversation. She got up, picked up her lunch bag, and then turned back, putting her hand on my shoulder. "You take care of yourself. So long, John."

"I will. So long."

Nothing is ever quite as it seems, and Cindi has never been an exception to that rule. In fact, you might say she has been the embodiment of that rule. We're all bound to eventually find someone who has been irrevocably misshapen by his or her past and who has been bent beyond the point of fixing. It is quite possible to bend a piece of metal, for example, until its integrity has been completely compromised. The fix is likely either a brace or a new piece of metal. With someone like Cindi, however, there is no brace which can be applied, nor is there any way to replace her. Everyone involved simply has to deal with her compromised integrity.

I have been dealing with Cindi for twelve years now. Childhood traumas, loss of basic trust in other people: once these things are gone, they don't come back. At least they didn't with Cindi. Misshaped and elusively hostile, she found the perfect opportunity in me, unprepared as I was and without any prior experience with someone like her.

Every one of us is a person – with good and bad characteristics. Deciding whether a characteristic is good or bad, however, can be…difficult…elusive…misleading. Good and bad can sometimes switch places on you when you aren't looking. And perhaps they never were as we believed to begin with.

The Sign

In 1997, I was just finishing college. I suppose I should have seen it coming about then. I really thought I was smarter than I was at the time. You would think after enough failed relationships (of which I'd had my share by age 22) I would have started to see some signs along the way. Maybe a red flag here or there. I probably did, too, but I never paid attention. I was usually hyper-focused on making the relationship work. How un-guy of me to say that, I know. I should be saying I wanted to get laid!

And I did. But that was only if the circumstance, the relationship, was right. I really wanted someone with whom I could be good friends and who would be crazy about me. I wanted someone with whom I could laugh and who would back me up when I needed it – someone who would catch me before I went too far one way or the other. But it wasn't just me, me, me! I was completely ready to reciprocate. I wanted to be a good boyfriend. I knew I could, too.

Up until then, however, things hadn't gone my way. For one reason or another, I couldn't find a girl who quite met my criteria or vice versa. Then along came Maggie, and she really made me wonder if perhaps things would be different with her. Well, not at first. At first, I didn't want to have anything to do with her. That's part of what made the relationship special. We had an interesting beginning which made the stuff that followed seem all the more amazing.

She had a huge crush on me during my senior year, but she just didn't seem to be my type; a little too forward maybe. Or maybe she was too into herself, or I didn't think she was pretty enough. It's hard to remember the exact reason. She was actually good looking. She had beautiful white skin and voluptuous curves that I could see would be fun to explore were I to get close enough. Her curly, dark hair, quick wit, and beautiful eyes were also alluring. But I didn't see any of that at first. I just saw some reason or another to not have anything to do with her. I can't even remember my thought process. Maybe I just was being contrary.

Whatever the reason, I avoided Maggie, but she always seemed to be lurking nearby, along with her request: let's go out. All year she plagued me. Finally, I decided to play a bit of a trick on her. I would have her come along with me and my pal Jake to a coffeehouse, and we would act annoying the whole time. That way, she could decide for herself that this wasn't going to work. I thought it was very clever.

She dropped everything when I called her and was in the lobby of Old Main in about ten minutes. I didn't know until later she had dropped her studying for an important test. I felt bad about it when I found that out, but at the time, I was getting a huge kick out of the plan. This annoying chick was about to get out-annoyed.

And she did. Maggie and I met Jake at a coffee shop called Uncommon Grounds in Uptown. It was spring in Minneapolis. The cold, icy winter was behind us, and the buds on the trees along Hennepin Avenue were growing big enough to burst. Hennepin Avenue was alive with bicycles, convertibles, motorcycles, and plenty of foot traffic. Street sweepers went by on the busy street, washing away all the salt and sand that had accumulated in the gutters from the city's war on ice that past winter. It seemed the entire population was experiencing the exuberance of being outside without having to wrap in several layers and rush to shelter with every step. The thrill of the color green on the trees and the sweetness in the air created an opportunity for the entire city to rejoice. We made it!

The little coffeehouse, offset from the street, sat behind its patio and budding shrubs. The chairs and tables had already been set out, and a few hardy coffee drinkers sat at a table outside in the cool air. An old man was out sweeping away the sidewalk sand and ice-melt that could now be cleared for summer. It was in the low 60s Fahrenheit, so we sat inside. Uncommon Grounds was actually a residential house that the owner had converted into a coffeehouse. There was enough room inside for the tables and chairs, yet it felt cozy at the same time. If we couldn't think of anywhere else to go, Uncommon Grounds was the default spot, always.

When Maggie and I got there that afternoon, Jake already had a table. We got our tea and coffee and sat down. Right away Jake and I started in with the dumb jokes. When I called him earlier, I just told him to act like we normally did when we were by ourselves, but exaggerated a little (very little) for Maggie. He knew what to do.

The plan was expertly executed. She didn't want to have anything to do with me or Jake after an hour or so of us acting like idiots. It was great! But then, as it often happens in stories worth retelling, the tables turned. As we were leaving, it hit me. I actually liked her. Maggie had surprised me by being cool and even politely laughing with us despite Jake's and my display of idiocy. Yet it was a bit too late for me to undo what we had done. The next time I called, I was turned down flat. Yes, Jake and I were that good. Still, I couldn't help myself; I had to try repairing the damage.

I did eventually remedy the situation. I won her over. It took a few months, but it was worth it. Later, we had a great story to tell about our romantic initiation. By the summer of 1997, I went to her house in Wisconsin while her family was gone, and we decided to get really serious. That's right; I was going to get laid! But don't think I took it as lightly as that sounds. I wanted to have a real, substantial, spiritual relationship. For the first time with any girl, I knew she and I had a shot at something profound. Sure, I had thought that before, but this time was different. This time I thought I had a girl who also wanted a very deep and stable relationship. That's always the point for me. Without that, the sex is crap. Getting to that point with someone like Maggie made everything that much more fulfilling. As a guy, I realize it's pretty lame of me to write that, but the truth ain't nothing but the truth. And that's the truth.

We got to the house, made some popcorn, put a VHS tape in the video player, and then she remembered something. She had almost forgotten to go back to her session at the Scientology place she attended. She had left something hanging in Downtown Minneapolis with some L. Ron Hubbard guru and had to go back. She had promised whoever it was she would show up that afternoon.

I know that sounds too funny to be true, but I was so surprised and taken aback I didn't know what to say, except, "Are you serious?" And she was! She dropped me off at the college an hour later, and I stood outside in the sunshine, smoking and walking on the concrete benches with wooden seats, confused. She went back for part two of some important session. I can't say I noticed a difference when she was done, but what did I know?

It was such a nice afternoon at the college: 70s and sunny. I could smell the grass being cut in the park. The day was wonderful except for how I was feeling. Maggie and I had come this far as a couple, and we had this really quiet, gentle time planned just for ourselves, away from the city, away from studying, away from everything but what mattered most: us. Now I was standing on a worn, wooden bench at school smoking cigarette after cigarette wondering whether 'us' mattered at all.

While I paced, my buddy Roland came by and said, "Hey John, what are you doing here? I thought you were out for the weekend." So I told him why I was walking around aimlessly on the benches.

He said, genuinely, only the way he can, "Dude, that really sucks. Sorry to hear about that." Then he added, almost as if he already knew the answer would be no, "We're playing tonight at the 400 Bar down the street. Bring your Rhodes and sit in. At least you'll have something fun to do."

Of course, I didn't. I still had a shot, after all, at reaching that unique place that two people can reach when they really click. I still had a shot, after Maggie's session, of getting what I so desperately had hoped for: a real girlfriend who would put her effort, heart, soul, and everything into the two of us. I still had a shot at getting laid too. The 400 Bar wouldn't know if I were there or not.

But to Maggie, the weekend was like a container into which several things could fit. I was one of those things; slightly less important than all the other things put together – slightly less important than everything else that pertained to her life – but one of the important things, nonetheless. She assured me of that. I figured with time and much effort on my part, my importance to her would grow. If I could put her first, make sure her needs were being met, she would eventually do the same for me. She would show me that I was more important than anything else going on in her life. I just had to hang in there.

At this point in my life, I was passing an important road sign that I was about to completely miss. After all, I was hoping to receive the behavior I alone was demonstrating in the relationship. It made perfect sense to me that eventually Maggie would put me first, above everything. Then the relationship would be mutual. Then the reciprocation would begin. I wanted to make the relationship work, and I knew I could, if only all by myself.

Even so, I stood there smoking impatiently, wondering whether I should just ditch her altogether or whether I could convince myself that, had I a check up with a doctor, I would have made her wait while I went in. I could convince myself that I wouldn't have called and rescheduled; I would have immediately left her somewhere and gone. I knew it wasn't true, but maybe, I thought, I could talk myself into it being true.

Frankly, waiting for her wasn't the problem, really. The problem was the effort I was making which wasn't matched. And it never would be. But there I was, efforting. Trying to squeeze my fists long enough and hard enough that I would finally make it work, if only all by myself. And since I thought that was possible, I missed that sign again and again.

The relationship flopped pretty hard after not very long. I think of it as relationship consumerism. Maggie liked keyboard players like me. I was cute, had a brain, and was fun. That got her down the road a ways. I was like a cool car to her. But eventually the alternator would crap out, the oil would need to be changed, there would be an unexplainable knocking sound coming from the engine, and she would realize that at the price of all those fixes, she could get a new keyboard player, a whole new vehicle to get her further down the road. This time, though, she could get one with a little more acceleration, a seat warmer, or whatever the new fancy would be. It's consumerism. I was consumed and was left on the roadside. And that was that.

After that was over, I finally decided to take up my buddy Roland on his offer to play a gig with his band. After that, I stuck with the band till the end. Actually, I probably had the most to do with the band breaking up, but that's getting a little ahead of the story at the moment. What pertains here is that I spent my time in that band missing the same road sign that I saw with Maggie, over and over and over. But the lesson is there to be learned and keeps coming back until you finally can't help but get it. There were plenty of subsequent relationships during which I could have noticed something was wrong right off the bat, but didn't.

In the beginning, the ease of meeting girls while playing with a band was such that I thought surely what I had failed to accomplish with Maggie would eventually present itself. I hoped and waited for it with plenty of girls. After all, the sheer variety of girls was more than I had ever encountered and in such a very short time. Statistically speaking, I figured I was bound to find the relationship I was seeking.

What I was about to find out, though, was that the sign I kept missing would soon whack me straight away, where it would hurt the most, where I couldn't help but run head-long into it, wheels screeching, my every effort to avoid it, finally not enough.

That metaphorical collision and subsequent careen into the abyss is now far enough in the rearview mirror that I have made a few personal discoveries since then, perhaps from the pain of thinking about these events for such a long time. The first lesson began to present itself with Maggie, but she was only the beginning.

From the Abyss   John Emil Augustine

Set Up

From 1997 through 2002, playing in the band became my main focus, but I also picked up hours with a landscaping company. What the landscaper allowed me to do, quite frankly, was leave the job any time I decided I had a good enough idea for a song or arrangement for the band. That wasn't in the official paperwork I signed, but that's what ended up happening, provided I did what I was asked every week. I didn't earn much, but the being-able-to-leave-anytime benefit for someone who has ideas come at anytime, anywhere more than made up for anything I endured on the job – even the times I was laid off for a while. Most of my arrangements for the band were written after I sped home trying desperately to remember a song idea long enough to get it on paper.

The problem with having that job was, of course, I didn't have much money. I lived with my buddy, Roland, and his now-wife, paying a very low rent until I decided I had worn out my welcome with his wife. In all fairness, I think she wasn't crazy about my cars. Yes, cars with an "s".

As you can imagine, when you live right at the poverty line, a car is not much of an option unless you do the work yourself when it breaks down. When you don't know much about cars and are learning as you go, you realize that having two cars is really the only way to go. Well, I realized that, anyway. Because if one car was out of commission, I could still drive the other one to work and back, come home, and start up where I left off fixing the other car until I had it running again. So I kept two cars at all times, one of which usually ran.

Actually, there were times when both were running, and I had to choose which one to drive. I remember one week in January 2000, when the band was on break. It was cold, below zero degrees that whole week, and most of the guys and their girlfriends had taken off to Roland's grandparents' cabin, almost everyone but me. I was girlfriendless at the time; the girls I met kept rolling in and then along again. Whoever *she* was, the girl with whom I hoped I could have a substantial relationship, I hadn't met her yet.

Anyhow, the girlfriend week at the cabin wasn't for single me, and I had no money for gas anyway.

The landscaping gig was cool, except that January there wasn't much for me to do. Even the maintenance guys I usually worked with had to tell me I couldn't help them that year because the union was cracking down, and I wasn't a member. So the money was thin. But there was an opportunity in another department.

The folks from the retail department loved me. Especially a woman named Emily. The whole department called me "The Duke" long after the inside joke had quit being funny. I had worked with an older guy who they called "The Landscape King," and therefore I was "The Duke." He didn't work there anymore. Only "The Duke" remained: me and my nickname. Emily made sure to perpetuate my nickname. It made us laugh. We all had a common bond, me and the retail department, so they asked me to help in the store. There was an opening, and they said they wished I would apply.

So I did. On Sunday night, while my pals were winter camping, I was alone in the house. My Taurus station wagon and Roland's Kia hatchback sat in front of the house (he had left me his keys just in case), and my own Dodge Omni hatchback was ready to go in the backyard. All three of them ran. However cold it got, I would make it to my Monday morning interview which was really just a formality. I was a shoe-in.

On Sunday night, I smugly thought about the awesome situation I was in. I was going to get to work with Emily, the coolest person I knew. The rest of the department was also awesome. I would walk in and, provided I did a good job and worked hard, would be viewed as a great addition. This was already going well.

I thought about the weather. It was supposed to be ten degrees below zero the next morning. I had plans A through C ready for the cold morning commute. It was such a good position to be in. The cold wouldn't affect my getting the coolest job ever. I had three cars at the ready.

"One car not starting tomorrow morning? Sure, that's possible," I thought to myself. My Taurus had trouble when it got below zero. I could see that not starting.

"Two cars not starting?" Ok, I had to admit there was an outside chance. I wasn't sure how good my battery was in the Omni. It might not start up. Two cars not starting was perhaps possible.

"But Roland's car not starting? Three cars not starting on the same morning? *I'd like to see that!*" The notion was not even remotely possible.

I liked my odds. I would be helping with the store before the week was out.

It was cold the next morning. The frost was thick on my bedroom window. Outside, it was the cold your nose wants to reject, the sharp pain in the nostrils that stings; lungs surprised by the sharp air coming in. I had no gloves. My sweatshirt under my Carhartt was my winter coat. But the car would be warm soon enough. Whichever car started.

The Taurus' bench seat was stiff with cold. The door creaked closed. My breath fogged the inside of the windshield as I turned the key and held it there, waiting. The engine growled slowly as I told myself, "No problem." My fingers on the metal ignition and metal key stung and burned as the low, even rr-rr-rr-rr slowed and stopped. This would not do. The Taurus was out.

So I crunched through the snow to the backyard. The Omni. The old, reliable Dodge Omni. I knew I had kept it for a reason. And here it was on a Monday morning in January: hero time for the Ol' Omni. The door groaned a low, terrible sound as I opened it. It had been a few weeks since I had fired it up. The seat cover felt strangely immobile. The clutch petal went slowly to the floor. The stick was in first, and I labored to get it into neutral.

"Oh boy. C'mon baby!" I whispered.

The engine had more life than the Taurus'. It jumped and sputtered as my numbing fingers clutched the ignition and key, holding onto the stinging metal I soon could not feel. I gave it a few pumps with the gas and off it went! Rrrrrrrrrrrroooom! Then the engine shuddered and quit.

Damn.

Again I turned the key, and the engine turned over under the hood.

Turned. Turned. Turned. Turned.

Turned. Turned. Turned.

Turned. Turned.

Turned.

Turned, but never fired again. "Flooded the goddamn thing," I growled under my breath. But wait...no need for cursing. In the back of my mind, I knew there was a plan C.

Two cars not starting, there was an outside chance, but three cars...

Roland's little hatchback sat behind the now-out-of-commission Taurus on the street. So I crunched through the backyard snow back to the street. I stooped into the front seat of the tiny Kia and backed the seat up to fit my legs, now feeling less and less of each extremity. Fumbling numbly for the key he had given me, I put it into the ignition.

I turned it and waited. My fingers no longer felt the metal ignition and key. My teeth began to chatter.

I waited a long time.

Down to my last car.

The engine shook. Fired. Shook. Fired again. Shook. Fired twice. Three times. Four.

"Oh please, you little car, come on...."

And

Then

Suddenly

Away it went, and I revved with everything my numb foot had. Rrrrrrrrrrrrrroooooooomm!!!!

"Yeaaaah! Three Cars Babyyyy!" I yelled from inside the bitter cold matchbox car that was about to save my butt.

I looked down at the dials. Everything was fine. Plenty of...crap! No gas! "Jesus, Stephen, how did you get this thing here so far below empty?" I muttered to myself, steaming the words as I stiffly put the car in reverse and backed away from the unresponsive Taurus. Thankfully, there was a gas station not two blocks away. Five bucks would do it. I turned the wheel and pulled forward into the street.

From the Abyss   John Emil Augustine

Down the road I sped, talking myself into having everything work out. "I can make some time on the freeway," I thought as I turned left into the gas station.

And then, silence.

Just me facing the gas station, pointed up hill, in a tiny car, halfway in the road and halfway on the sidewalk, and in no way closer to getting to my appointment on time. "What the hell?" I muttered. I turned the key. The engine turned over and over and over and over…

Of course! The tilt up the little hill into the gas station driveway made the car think it was completely out of gas. Or maybe it was. Either way, before I knew it, I was running down the adjacent alley back to the house because we had a gas can stashed in the garage. My ears felt like they were being pinched by dozens of mini-vices. My hands in my pockets made it hard to run, not to mention the ice-covered alleyway. Still, I got back as quickly as I could and bought my five bucks worth of gas, dumped it into Stephen's stranded car, and off I sped.

I was supposed to be starting my interview, but I had just entered the freeway. I would be twenty minutes late. This was quite a story. Holy shit, how crazy was this? Wait. This was too crazy. This was the kind of story an interviewer might hear when an interviewee was late. This was *exactly* the story they would hear. But mine was real! How could I make this sound real? After all, it was the only story I had. What else would I tell them? I had to tell them what happened. It wasn't an excuse, it was a reason. Boy, this was going to be tough to frame in my favor. Boy, they were really going to hear a whopper. I wished I could downsize it somehow.

But I really couldn't under the pressure of the quiet, hot, stale office room. So I told my whopper. What else could I do? I said this was the perfect story to use as an example of a story not to use when one is late for an interview. I knew that. I told them it was the only story I had. But in the end, because I had not called in the panic of trying to get to the interview, my mistake was a deal-breaker to the higher-up guy who was part of the interview team. I didn't get the gig. Some chick from another garden store got my shoe-in job. What could I say? I was completely bummed. I guess I learned the hard way to call ahead when late for an appointment.

Later that March, I found out who the new lady was. Candy or Cindi…something like that. I immediately hated her. Well, not really, but she kind of took my job, and now she would be a constant reminder of that in the break room three times a day.

And she was. Every time she'd come down the stairs with the rest of the crew, there was my job in walking, breathing, personified form. I hated that. She was nice enough, but I didn't talk to her very much. I sat somewhere else.

My friend, Emily, understood. We talked quite a bit. I still admired her from afar. She was so beautiful, so funny, so genuine. Looking at her was like looking at heaven; like seeing an angel. Her smile, her strawberry curls, her gorgeous eyes, and her sweet voice were wonderful beyond words.

One day we were both walking behind the store, and I said, "Hey, Emily, can I ask you a question?"

"Yes, of course."

"It's kind of personal. You don't have to answer."

She stopped. "You can ask me personal questions. You're The Duke…*and* you're John. You can talk to me."

"Ok, here goes. Were you always like this?"

"What?"

"Well, I meet so many girls, but none of them are like you. Maybe they are still too young. Were you different, say, ten years ago?"

She thought about it. "No, I was pretty much like this."

"Ok, that's good to know."

"Such a strange question."

"Well, you're so smart and pretty. So…together. I'm just hoping to get some clues on what I want to look for when I'm out meeting girls."

"John, you just made my week!" she said with a huge smile. "If I were single, I would ask you out."

"You just made *my* week, Emily!" We laughed. God, she was beautiful. *She* would ask *me* out? Hell, she had just made my year. I really admired her. Her laugh, her hair, her smarts, her smile. It wasn't sexual necessarily, and not love really, just admiration. She was so cool. I wished for my own version of her.

She knew I was still bummed about not getting the job, and now she knew what I was looking for romantically. And she also knew something else. Cindi, the new chick, had the hots for me. So Emily did a very cool thing. She set up a little party at her house for the people in her department and wouldn't take no for an answer from me. I *had* to come. I agreed to go to her house that Friday. She was the kind of person who I just couldn't say no to.

None of us knew it at the time, but I was being set up big time.

From the Abyss   John Emil Augustine

A Good Start

It was spring. After work, I drove to the party at Emily's house in Minneapolis. She had invited the whole store, including Cindi. Her house was beautiful, in the old craftsman style with quality woodwork and windows without argon. Doors that were not hollow inside and had sturdy, brown-brass knobs. Beautiful real hardwood floors bordered by oak mop boards.

There was food. There was beer and wine. There was herb, which really surprised me – these 30-somethings with weed. When it was time to go, bathed in numb happiness and cloudy anticipation, I walked the new chick, Cindi, to her car. She told me Emily was planning another get-together, and she wanted my number so she could call me with details. So I gave it to her; wrote it down on a receipt in her car.

She called me the next day, not about Emily's upcoming party, but just to say hi. I was finally a shoe-in. Everything was happening right on time. I no longer cared about not getting the store job. It was just great to be part of the gang; Emily's gang. Next, we all went out and had all you can eat crab at Joe's Crab Shack. It had first come to the Twin Cities about then. Emily kept scheduling little get-togethers for the store girls, their husbands, and, of course, me and Cindi.

And all of it worked. Cindi and I were soon inseparable. She was thin and fit. Not gorgeous, but pretty. Her nose was a little askew; there was a little bump on the bridge which was sexy to me. She had a front tooth that was bent in a way that reminded me of one of the moms from my old neighborhood whose eight year old daughter I was in love with at age four. In her own way, Cindi reminded me of a long time ago, of carefree summers, of Big Wheels and playing *The Wizard of Oz* on rainy days.

Cindi was 31. I was 25. It didn't matter. It never does when you are starting out. I just went with the traffic, followed the road ahead. Eventually, I was invited to her apartment. We sat and drank wine, listened to music, and talked. When we had run out of words, I asked, "Do you want to kiss me?" She said yes. It wasn't long after that I would wake up in her bed every morning, and the two of us would go to work together to the excited approval of the whole store who felt they had a hand in this fortunate turn of events.

Cindi's body was like a model's. That's what I told her, and it really was. I had never been with a woman so sleek and perfect. I adored every inch. She thought her boobs were too small, but I told her they were just right. I could cup them perfectly in my hand. They were soft, warm, tender pillows. This was our pillow talk. But the pillow talk was about to take an unexpected turn, and I had no idea what curves I would be led down.

Sometimes, I think I would like to go back and fix what I did; take the off-ramp. But you just never get to do that. Not really. Maybe you wouldn't want to. Because those signs keep showing up until you understand what is written. If not then, it would have hit me at another time. I saw the sign but didn't realize what it meant. And in fairness to me, there was no way I could have known. You can only really, truly see the future when it's in the past.

The Deal Breaker...Or Not

We were in bed one night in Cindi's apartment. It was raining. We turned off the TV and were quietly lying there, and she said, "I think I had better tell you something. This could be a deal breaker, but you have to know before we go too much farther."

I have to tell you, by 2000, I had heard very similar speeches in plenty of beds. It's sad, but that's how it was. Sign after sign in the rearview mirror, unread. I never asked for a second chance. I just knew that was that.

So I figured I was about to get half-way dressed, grab my toothbrush, or not, and drive home wondering what had happened this time. I sat up in bed, ready to listen but also ready to turn on the light and locate my clothes.

"Something happened to me when I was eight," she began. "I was raped."

Silence.

"It was my grandpa."

Silence.

Yikes. This was a new one for me. My heart raced. My fingers tingled. I was light-headed. I looked at the window's dripping darkness. Now what? I looked down at the comforter, at my bare stomach. I guessed I had to do something.

But what? Locating my clothes in silence seemed to be an insensitive move. "Well..." I said quietly, my throat not quite ready to make sounds. I bit both my lips and crossed my arms, hands grabbing my forearms. They were sweating. Cold. My feet were wet. Also cold. I couldn't move. Paralysis set in.

Shaking out of it, I tried to begin again. "I'm sorry to hear that." My throat was dry. I sounded different than I normally did. Whose voice was this? I shifted in the bed. "That sounds awful," I choked. Should I run? Is this something that is ok now? I had no idea how to assess the situation objectively. I had to make a split-second decision. Should I stick it out? How bad could it be?

There was more. She guessed she had better tell me the rest.

From the Abyss   John Emil Augustine

The rest? Where was this night going to end up? Is this what happened to the last guy? Did he hear this speech? I had seen a picture of him, sitting in her living room playing video games. Mulroony? That name was written in permanent marker on her cooler under the sink in the kitchen. She said he had left her and had not told his mom about it. Cindi had called his mom, and his mom had not known anything about their break-up. What had happened? Had he sneaked away as I was wishing I could do?

Suddenly my heart raced faster, and it felt like the room was getting smaller. Could I still slip out into the night beyond the wet window glass at which I stared blankly? The toothbrush could stay! I could slide, shaking, into my Omni, fire it up, put it in first, and be a block away in about a minute, tops. I longed for that sequence of events as I sat paralyzed in her bed about to undergo something I knew I would not like. How could I pause her? Distract her? Make her go into another room while I went through the front door in my underwear? If I just took my shoes, my only pair, I would get back ok and put other clothes on when I was safe. She could keep my pants like she kept the cooler from Mulroony. But what more could there be? Wasn't the first bit of information bad enough? The rest couldn't possibly be that bad.

Could it?

But this is life, I decided, and I had to tough this out. I had to listen. We were getting serious. Cindi was fine. She was ok now. Emily liked her, had even recommended her. She was a normal, functioning person who had worked through this, whatever it was. That was what was important. I could help her. I could be a good boyfriend. I could stand by her, whatever the situation. I could be the guy who stayed.

Couldn't I?

The Real Deal-Breaker

So the rest of the story was that her childhood hadn't been great. Her dad finally had enough, I guess, and convinced the family it would be a good idea to hit the road and live in an RV. So they sold the house, packed up Cindi and her two brothers, and headed to California. Once they got there, they got set up at a campsite, and the next morning her dad was gone. They didn't see him for twenty years.

In the meantime, they moved back to Minnesota. Her mother worked long hours. The kids looked out for themselves and Cindi's mom came home late at night. I guess all that about sealed the trust issue for her. She told me she had a very hard time trusting people. Then I began to see it firsthand.

First it was Emily. She suddenly hated Emily, and they had words. Emily found another position, a bit higher up, and Cindi was even angrier that the position had not been offered to her. They never talked again. Then it was Lisa who took over the department. Cindi had always liked her, but one day, bam! Lisa did something Cindi didn't like, and ever after she felt that Lisa was against her. It went all the way through the department – one at a time, all her coworkers became a problem.

She began to act differently at home too. No sex anymore. Not much talking. Only anger. Every night when we drove home, she was mad about something. I tried to find things she would like doing on the weekends, hoping she would get through the phase and get back to being Cindi. "Being Cindi." Huh! I had no idea what that meant.

Still, I was willing to hang in there. I wanted to be the guy who was different; who *would* be there to help – not just a name on a cooler. I knew it might not be easy. I knew that I had no idea what I was getting myself into. I knew I might even fall flat. Yet I also knew I could be patient. I could be loving. I knew I could guide when necessary and could stand by my word.

Cindi sometimes did get back to the way I knew her originally. Once in a while she snapped out of it, and we were back to where we had left off. Except, I had this picture of her childhood ever in my mind, and she knew I did. I kept thinking about what she had said.

As a kid, she had basically raised her brothers. They hated her. *Still.* It was very strange to experience a family dynamic I had never anticipated nor previously experienced. Her relationships were confusing to me. How she determined who was in favor, I just couldn't tell. It seemed like it switched, slowly, around the circle of those with whom she was acquainted. She didn't trust anybody for long; that soon became clear.

Could I blame her? What a tough trip she'd had up to this point. So I watched the who's-in-who's-out roundabout continue and meanwhile questioned our relationship again and again. It was a tough place to be. I was trying. I was happy when she was sad. I was cool-headed when she was raging mad. I was up-beat when she was in bed, not wanting to face a day. I could be those things, her yang's ying. Never tiring. A salve to ease her suffering. But the curve balls came in steadily, never with a hint of where they were going. I stood up to the plate for every pitch, carefully timing my swings, intelligently learning when to let certain pitches go by. Occasionally we'd get into a bad place, and I wouldn't know what to do in the newest situation, struggling confusedly with her erratic emotional outpourings.

I don't know why, but by mid-summer Cindi did seem to snap out of her anger for a longer period, and our relationship again picked up and became happier; things were getting back to what I had hoped they would be…to what I had hoped for since I had been with Maggie. We were really enjoying our time together. Weekends were back to being a time for outdoor fun: hiking, climbing, sex in the woods, cooking together, little wine parties in the bathtub, just the two of us. We would see the occasional movie or concert. She came to all my shows. It was exciting. In the interim, the brief moments during which the anger against someone had abated and before it focused on the next, I thought, "Hey, we're really cookin'." But it was only for brief snippets.

Then it happened. It was my turn. She had gone around the circle enough times that finally, after being skipped over however many times, finally I could not be skipped again. It was my turn.

I remember playing a gig at the Uptown Bar in Minneapolis. The guys and I sound checked while the place was empty and then had a bite to eat before the crowd trickled in. The Uptown bar didn't have the greatest sound system in the Twin Cities. In fact, it was my least favorite bar in terms of sound. There was only a mono system in the house. It was just a stack of speakers on stage left. The stage itself was fairly small, but it was enclosed, so you couldn't miss-step and fall off either side. The room was long and narrow, and the stage was at the far end. Tables flecked the floor, and booths bordered it.

Adjoining that room was a second room with similar dimensions but with more booths and the bar. That part I liked because you could be next door listening to the show at a lower volume while getting a bite to eat and having a conversation. The food was great, so despite the sound limitations, it was a cool hangout, and people loved to go there.

The band was at full steam, and everyone knew a crowd was guaranteed at every gig, everyone but me. I remembered gigs when we'd just started out. Back then it was not uncommon to have a three person audience, all three of whom were our girlfriends. It was my constant fear that no one would show up. I was always apprehensive during that time after sound check and before the room filled. As it began to fill that night at the Uptown, I went around talking to the people who were there to see us. I really did appreciate their being there, and I always made sure to let them know.

Cindi came through the door with a few of the other guys' girlfriends. She had my leather jacket on, which was pretty cool. This was a good life, I thought. I went over to her, kissed her, and chatted a little. She had found the place ok. She had parked where I recommended. She wanted a drink. I got through that conversation and had her squared away with the girlfriends while I went and said hi to more people who had come. I was always surprised that they came, that they brought their friends, that some had just heard about the band and had come. I never got used to that. I almost thought we were cheating them out of a good time, but in truth we *were* the good time. We were the excuse to get out and scream, get drunk, hug each other, hook up, and all that.

We had a good show. The crowd in that recording is almost louder than the band, and in all the right places. We premiered an arrangement I had written: the first one I wrote with no instrument on hand, just sitting at Cindi's dining room table with a pencil. I remember being surprised I could do that. It was an exciting time. So much fun. Things coming together. Careless was the life. The days were sunny, the nights warm. Everyone existed in a happy state, together.

I had to go back to our drummer's house in North Minneapolis the night we played at the Uptown Bar. I was still renting a room from Stephen even though I hardly ever slept there. The next night, we were to be on the radio, and we needed to rehearse during the day so we could get an acoustic song or two ready to play live in the KQRS studio. More excitement!

After rehearsing at Stephen's that afternoon, I called Cindi to see how she was and to ask her to record us on the radio that night with her boombox. She said she didn't think she would.

"What? No, you have to. I want to hear what we sound like."

"I don't want to." Her voice was cold. There was a lot of silence.

"Hello?"

"I'm here," she said.

"You're really not going to listen tonight?"

"I doubt it."

"Why?"

"Why do you think, John?"

"Tired?"

"Yeah, I'm tired all right."

"You could take a nap this afternoon."

"No, you know what? I'm tired of you not contributing."

"Huh?"

"You heard me. Don't tell me you don't know what I'm talking about. You didn't spend more than ten minutes with me last night."

"But I was playing."

"You could have stayed with me before you played. All the other guys were sitting with their girlfriends. And you were off walking around, flirting, yacking it up like you wanted to avoid me with every molecule of your body."

"What? I went to say hi to people. I talked with you plenty. I don't get it."

"Oh, I'm sure you don't cause your way is always the way we do things."

"It is?"

"Fuck you."

"*What?*"

"You heard me! I am so sick of this!" I could hear the words forced past her vocal cords, gritty and distorted.

"Oh, ok I get it. I understand. Hey, I just didn't really realize that, I guess."

"Oh yeah, that's a great answer. You're great at coming up with just the right answer, aren't you, John?"

"*What?*"

"That's what I thought."

The absurdity of the conversation confused me. But this was a simple situation really. Actually, an easy fix was possible.

"Well, next time, I'll just hang out with you and not walk around. I can do that. I'm just used to saying hi to everyone. That's all."

"Next time? That's great. Let's plan on that for next time, John."

"Ok. Wait, are you being sarcastic?"

Her next statement, strangely, came to an abrupt crescendo. "You'll just have to wait till next time, *won't you!*"

Click.

My adrenaline was really going at that point. What the hell had just happened? Was I really that bad? I guessed I was. Boy, I really thought I was much less insensitive. I couldn't believe I'd been so oblivious. What had I been thinking? I was living it up while Cindi was having an awful time.

I was self-centered. It was that simple. I was thinking about myself and the band when I should have been concentrating on her. It really was that simple. I was like a selfish child only concerned with *my* music and *my* band. Cindi must have felt like such an afterthought. Here I'd been thinking everything was going along so smoothly, but the whole time she was harboring resentment.

I was a stereotypical musician, really. Completely self-absorbed. Sure, I paid some attention to Cindi. It seemed to me like I was doing a good job of being a boyfriend. I wrote her some songs. She loved them. But writing songs was not enough, of course. Going on dates was not enough. Even during the dates I would think about music. What I decided was I had to make things more about Cindi, not about me or my music. I had to quit thinking of myself. Maybe I was like Maggie in my own way, fitting Cindi into the swell of things I had going on in my life, but not putting her first or above everything else.

I tried to stop thinking about it long enough to get through the radio gig, tried to sound happy like everything was cool, tried to forget how selfish I was for that hour on the radio. The KQ studio was fun. They had coffee and rolls for us in the break room. We were handed a list of words we could not say on air, and we all stood around by the vending machines, nervously talking and getting caffeinated.

Once we were on air, it was odd not to actually see an audience. Mei Young's smooth, sexy voice guided us through questions, stories, and a few acoustic songs. Then we were done. I went back to Stephen's where I fell asleep thinking of Cindi and my predicament. It was a caffeinated, nervous sleep.

I woke up early thinking that I simply had to patch this up. Things had been going so well. I would have to put myself in check and somehow fix the problem. Wait, this was an easy fix. I could simply become more aware of what I was doing and not think so much about myself. I had it all worked out by time I ate breakfast at ten the next morning.

I went over to Cindi's that afternoon and knocked on the door. She opened it but left the chain on. I talked through the crack. I said I was an idiot, said I had not paid enough attention. She calmed down and invited me in. We sat and watched TV. She was quiet. I thought I would be able to stay the night and go into work with her like usual. But I was not invited. I asked if I should go home. She said I should do what I wanted. I wasn't being rejected, but I wasn't being welcomed back. I was in a sort of relationship purgatory. Wait, I was in the proverbial dog house! I got it. I was to go away for a while because I was in the *dog house*. Ah! It made so much sense. I could deal with this, I thought.

I went back to Stephen's for the night. I went to work the next day and was avoided. I went home after work and called Cindi. She didn't want to see me; didn't want to talk to me.

"Hmmm…this may not be the dog house. This may be it," I thought.

I decided to leave her alone for a while. Absence makes the heart grow fonder, right? I hoped. Actually, in a way I hoped not. My emotions were becoming mixed.

Friday that week, I got a call. I was to come over. Cindi needed to talk. Ah-ha! This was the let-down; the final word in the break-up. This was her dumping me. This would actually be good, I reasoned, because the relationship was getting a little weirder than I had anticipated. I would accept the dumping and move on. It was best for both of us, I realized. She was not being rejected, she was rejecting. She would feel pretty good about this, too, I reasoned. I was beginning to get a feeling of peace as I pulled up to her apartment for the last time.

I looked around the side of her building. We had sat there on the steps one warm July night, just talking. It had been such a nice night. So care-free. No expectations. Just hanging out because we liked each other. Inside, the stairs led up to the second floor. I used to pat her, very sneakily, on the butt while following her up those stairs. It was mischievous fun, and it made her giggle. Once again, I heard the familiar creaks of the boards as I climbed the stairs. This would be the last time I would hear them. What had I left here that she would hand me? A toothbrush. Maybe some clothes. Underwear for sure. They had been in the wash a week before. A jar of peanut butter maybe.

I knocked. From inside, she said it was open, so I walked in. Cindi was sitting on the couch. I sat down in the chair. "Well, here it is," I thought. "Hope it happens quickly so I can get back and watch the Twins game."

"Where do you think our relationship is at right now?" She sounded mad.

"Well, I think you're going to break up with me, if that's what you mean."

"I was going to."

"Ok."

"But what if I weren't? Then what?"

"Well, I think we would have a shot at making things better, but it would take a lot of work on my part, I guess. Why, you don't want to break up?"

"Let me show you something."

"Ok."

She went into the other room, back to our bedroom. That is, her bedroom. My former bedroom.

"This is a slightly weirder break-up than I had anticipated," I thought to myself as I sat there alone. "Maybe I should just say I need a break and leave it at that. That might be a really good idea. If she gets mad, I can just leave and say, 'call me later,' and then she won't." I had a little plan – this was good.

She came back to the living room with something in her hand. Blue and plastic. Small. It was some kind of tube. She was giving me a…tampon? What was this?

She handed it to me. There was writing on it. Some kind of crude little window with two lines in it. I was completely baffled.

"What is it?"

"It's a pregnancy test."

I quit breathing and stared at it.

"I'm pregnant."

Surprise

Sitting in Cindi's living room at age 25, I looked at the pregnancy test and let Cindi's words sink in. Then I realized my life as I knew it was about over. Although this had happened to our drummer once. He had told his girlfriend he wasn't ready for a baby. She was so relieved that she immediately went out and got an abortion. Problem solved. I figured it was worth a try. I know it sounds cruel, but I was in complete denial.

Cindi explained that she had already had an abortion and was not about to do that again. I can't say I was relieved, but I admired her conviction. Actually, it was reassuring in a way. Still, walking into what would otherwise have been a break up and then hearing that I was going to be a dad created an extreme mixture of emotions. I honestly wasn't sure quite what to say or do about it.

I'm not sure people actually think of the dad in such a situation other than about what he would do to help the mom. To be fair, a lot of dads, for whatever reason, end up out of the picture as a result of situations like this one. The mom is going to care for the child; that tends to be a given. What about the dad who is out of favor with the mom? Well, there are weekends, Father's Day, Christmas and Easter. Well, maybe not Easter. Perhaps sometime during teacher conference week. As long as the money comes in, the dad can be quite overlooked. Again, a lot of dads are actually cool with that arrangement and want even less time with the kid. That's probably partly why things are the way they are in the world when it comes to many people's perception of dads.

I do believe, however, there exists an ability which dads exhibit but which nobody ever actually mentions, and that is "Paternal Instinct." I believe it exists. I know I have experienced it in my dad, grandfathers, and even some older coworkers I have known. You know Paternal Instinct when you experience it, though it is hard to narrow down a definition. The definition is somewhat elusive, though I have made a few personal observations about Paternal Instinct in my 37 years.

From the Abyss   John Emil Augustine

Paternal Instinct is different than Maternal Instinct. And it is hard for me to put my finger on a valid description of either set of traits. You might give some examples such as mothers tend to be nurturing, and fathers tend to be challenging. Mothers tend to demonstrate emotional strength; fathers, old-fashioned know-how. Dads tend to give kinesthetic advice, perhaps pertaining to machinery; moms tend to give relational advice. And those descriptions might work in one set of cases but not in another. So you can generalize to a point about the differences, and then the definition, almost realized, will slip through your fingers. Truly, there is nothing necessarily mutually exclusive to dads and moms in terms of traits they exhibit, yet there is a palatable and knowable difference. You know it when you experience it.

So perhaps it is better to say that dads exhibit, generally, their own versions of traits for their children to observe and practice that are different from moms' versions. I have no doubt there is a difference. An extensive continuum is probably necessary to graph such differences as they pertain to mothers and fathers, and this is not the place for it. Regardless, the real difference, in my experience, is that mothers are more likely, in general, to actually model the traits. The dads who do, in their own dad way, have Paternal Instinct; they take their children into account. Accounting for the child is the important part of both Maternal *and* Paternal Instinct. That, I realized, is what I needed to do at that moment: take this very, very tiny baby that I couldn't even see yet, into account.

But I had nine months. I decided I needed a day or two to make all of this work in my head. I had to come up with some sort of plan and present it – another kind of dad thing, perhaps. I didn't have to steer the ship, but I had to be ready to assist somehow. I told Cindi I would help however I could to make this work out, but I needed a few days to get things squared away in my own life. She said she understood. I really just needed to adjust to the idea before I did anything. Like being in a car crash. I needed a little time just to absorb what had happened.

And I did. It took two days, and then I had a plan. I went back and asked whether or not she would let me help. It seemed like an appropriate first question. I told her I would help in whatever way possible. She was actually relieved. Her whole demeanor changed back to the Cindi I had first known, and I was exuberantly relieved to see her change. I told her we could make it fun. We could be whatever version of a family we wanted as long as we worked together. She liked that. During that conversation, we had grown closer.

The next day, I called my mom and asked to meet her at her office. I told her what was going on and that I needed help. First order of business: picking out a surprise engagement ring. I had a pretty good idea Cindi would go for the idea of marriage, and I asked my mom to help me find a suitable ring. I got a store card at some place in the mall, and before I knew it, I was all set up to make payments at some crazy rate like 24%. What a rip-off. But I didn't really know that at the time. I just knew I was going over to Cindi's to surprise her. This was going to be fun!

When I got to the apartment, her girlfriend was there, and they were about to watch a movie. I said I could come back, but they asked me to watch, too. It was *Erin Brockovich*. I still hate that movie, but not because of the movie itself. Before I had gotten to Cindi's apartment, I had stashed the ring box in my back pocket and then hid the large lump under my coat. When I was talked into watching the movie, I sat down on the damn ring box, removed my coat, and put it on my lap to otherwise hide it. Between sitting for two hours on a ring box and sweating because the coat was making me hot, I remember thinking I would never see that movie again because it had been too painful to watch…physically!

When we were finally alone, I said a quick little speech about how much I loved her and knew our relationship would need work but that I wanted to be there for her and the baby. I told her I would make this work as smoothly as I possibly could. She was relieved I hadn't run. She told me she had expected I would abandon her. She was also relieved to have my full support. She of little faith! She wasn't too sure about my current job. What else could I do?

The next order of business was finding myself a real job. A friend of Cindi's recommended a local college which happened to be hiring English teachers. I walked into the interview with my stage clothes, a Bachelor's degree, and the promise to start my

Master's. The department chair, Heidi, loved me despite my lack of experience. As she was leaning toward me, she called Cindi's friend and asked her why she should give me the job. I don't know what Cindi's friend said, but before I knew it, I was sitting in the HR office signing something I had never seen before: health insurance forms. I didn't want to teach and didn't really even want to be a dad, but I knew I would be good at both. And, for the most part, I was.

We got married three months later in the fall. Cindi was only showing a little, and once they let the dress out, no one could tell. We waited to break the news about the baby to the rest of the family so that everyone could focus on the wedding first, letting that be the important thing before all attention switched to the baby. In the end, we had some grandparents who were a little taken aback by the order of events, but everyone eventually came around.

That year we could not afford a tree for Christmas. Everything had happened so fast that we ended up being very poor for a few months. We were prepared for everything, it seemed, except that detail. So we bought a few spruce boughs on sale the day before Christmas. The smell alone, piney and wintery, made everything feel that much happier. We bunched and tied the boughs together and hung them on the apartment wall. Underneath, we put Cindi's childhood stocking and the two new stockings her mom made; one for me and one for the baby. Then we pointed the camera at ourselves and set it to shoot.

Somewhere that picture is tucked, unless it has since been thrown away, between random things in a dirty cardboard box, perhaps in an attic or basement. The earth has circled the sun twelve times since then, and twelve times the cold Minnesota winters have melted into beautiful, warm summers. And that photo, a little over twelve years old, if it has survived, documents the last time Cindi and I were truly happy together.

The Slow Drag

Not that we were completely happy by the time Christmas rolled around. Things that led up to it were allusions to a scary turn of events about to come.

To start, my mom had offered to pay for a lot of the wedding festivities. That meant she wanted to have a say about almost everything: the church, the reception, the decorations, the parties leading up to the wedding. To her credit, she did a lot of the legwork in addition to paying. I thought it was great because I could concentrate on my new job, and Cindi could concentrate on…well…getting angry.

Cindi didn't really have a plan or want to do the work, but she did want to criticize my mom's choices and attempts to help. If Cindi had originally planned on having a certain kind of wedding, I never knew. Trying to drag out of her what she actually wanted was impossible. She just knew what my mom was doing was not what she wanted. I tried to get her to voice her concerns at least to me, but it just wasn't happening. She simply ended up being pissed off at my mom. It was hard for her to let go of that feeling; several years would need to pass.

Work was also starting to piss her off. She felt that Lisa, the lady in charge of the store, was against her. I don't think she was, but that's how Cindi saw it. Cindi was mad about almost everything that happened in the store. I told her to bring things up with her coworkers, but she kept silent and let the anger grow. Her grievances were building, and her coworkers didn't seem to be too excited to work with her anymore. But I didn't feel sorry for them because I was the one who had to live with her.

Just before the wedding, the band threw me an insane bachelor party, complete with a bus and all the strip clubs and booze we could handle. At one point, the guys got me on stage, and about ten dancers had me sit in a chair. One at a time, each girl stood on my thighs, balancing in her crazy-high-heels, and then slammed herself down into a sitting position on my lap. It hurt!

I asked one girl, "Doesn't that hurt your legs?" She said no.

I found it so strange that the guys had taken up a collection for that kind of dance! Afterward, they said they didn't know the girls were going to do that either.

Later we went back to Stephen's, and the guys ended up wrestling me in the backyard. The trombone player picked me up at one point and slammed me down onto my feet. It was not a bad thing to do because we were having fun, but the knee I had once torn in 9th grade finally gave out after all the night's punishment. When I hit the ground, I felt it pop. Something had gone wrong inside my knee. I crawled out from under the pile and assessed the situation.

My drunken band mates wanted to continue the craziness, but I knew I was in trouble. I sneaked out the gate, limped to my car, and took off. My knee could still handle pushing the clutch, but the whole leg was beginning to throb terribly. I didn't have much time.

I got home and stumbled into the shower while Cindi woke up and asked what we had done. I told her, "I never want to go to a strip club ever again!" Then she saw me hobble out of the shower and drag myself to the bed.

"What is wrong with your leg?" she asked.

"I think I popped my knee somehow. It hurts. Do we have any Advil?"

Cindi was suddenly furious. She would not go back to bed. She would not be in the same room as I was. She didn't even want to be in the apartment with me. I tried to tell her the guys and I had been wrestling, and it was an accident. But an accident was not a good explanation to her. She acted like it was the worst thing I could have possibly said.

Then Cindi began to vacuum which was her angry ritual. I was so tired. I fell asleep despite the commotion. When I'd finally fallen into a good sound sleep, she woke me up to yell at me. How could I do this? How did I expect to participate in the wedding? Didn't I know how bad this was? "Get up! Get up!" she kept yelling.

Eventually I did what she said and stood up, naked and on one leg. She told me to try to stand on the other leg, so I did. Instantly, the pain shot up to my neck, and I dropped to the bed.

"You useless idiot!" she screamed. "What am I going to do? *What is wrong with you?*"

I was speechless. Tired and spaced out, I lay back down and covered up. I had to sleep. Every once in a while, perhaps in reality, perhaps in my dream, I heard her yell, "You motherfucker!" as I slept with the bedroom light on.

When I awoke, Cindi was in the living room. I used a stool like a walker to get to the bathroom. My knee was swollen. She walked into the bathroom as I sat there peeing and started up again. The anger was overwhelming. Was there more to this that I wasn't getting? Was this really so bad for the wedding – for her? Walking down the aisle would be possible with a crutch. Teaching would be possible. Everything else would be unaffected. What was I missing? I had insurance to see a doctor. Driving would be tough with a stick, though. Pushing down the clutch had become a non-option. But I could trade cars with someone for a while. I could drive somehow. If only I had crutches. That was it!

"Hon, can you bring me the phone? My mom has my old crutches from high school. I want to call her and see if I can get them."

But Cindi was back in the other room and did not answer.
"Hon?"
Nothing.
"Honey!"
Nothing.
"Cindi!"
"I am not going to talk about this," came her cold reply.
"I need some crutches. My mom has some!"
Nothing.
"Can I have the phone?"

"Ugh. This is not going well," I thought. I gingerly pulled on some pants, grabbed my stool, and walked myself out to the dining room phone. I got to a chair and picked up the phone. By the time I hung up, my mom was on her way, and Cindi had taken my stool.

"Can I get my stool back, please?"
"Why don't you come get it."
"What?"
Silence.

So I dragged myself across the hardwood floor, on my side, back to bed. I didn't know what was happening to Cindi, but I hoped she would snap out of it soon. At least, I figured, my mom was on her way with some crutches. I would be mobile soon enough.

But Cindi refused to answer the door when she arrived. My mom called and called from downstairs. No answer. I began to drag my body toward the apartment door. I figured I could slide down the stairs. But when Cindi saw me sliding across the floor, she finally went to answer the door. What would happen? Cindi hated my mom. My poor mom was walking into a very bad situation. But Cindi didn't let her in. She just grabbed the crutches and brought them up. I was sitting on the floor in the living room when she opened the door and threw them at me. I hoisted myself up, put the crutches under my armpits, and went out the door. I heard her yell as I began down the stairs, "Don't come back!"

I didn't feel like it, that was for sure.

Somehow I was able to operate the clutch, brake, and gas with one foot. It was awkward, but I got the hang of it. I took off to my folks' and got there a few minutes after my mom. My mom said Cindi had looked very angry at the door. My mom had tried to tell her, "Boys will be boys," but it hadn't seemed to help.

I got the name of the knee guy I had seen back in high school and discovered he was still in business. I made an appointment, and my dad offered to trade cars for a few weeks. An automatic made all the difference. Now I was in good shape, considering.

I managed to smooth things over with Cindi. The next day, she drove me to the knee doctor and he felt my knee with his fingers. He told me if I got rid of the crutches and began to walk very carefully on the knee, it would be fine. Nothing was torn. I only limped slightly when I walked down the aisle a few weeks later. Things were back to normal…kind of.

A few weeks after the wedding, I got a call during class. It was Cindi, and it was an emergency. I called a break and got on the phone. There was a situation at work. She was furious. I could hear her voice shaking. They had not let her in the store that morning. Only one person was in the building, and she had knocked for 20 minutes before whoever it was heard her. Someone had left the door locked accidentally, but Cindi was sure it had been intentional. She was screaming as she told me. I was completely confused. This was the situation I stopped class for? This was getting ridiculous.

"Well, if you think it's that bad, quit." That would make the point, I thought.

"Fine!" She hung up.

When I got home that night, she told me she had taken my advice and quit her job that morning. She told Lisa, her supervisor, everything she had complained to me about for the last six months, and then she walked off the job.

I was shocked. I couldn't understand how anything that had happened at her job could possibly be that bad. They were such a good group of coworkers. But that was that, and we were now down to my income. Cindi was pregnant and unemployed. Not a good combination. Thank goodness for my insurance.

To be fair, I had my faults and had contributed to our problems by that point to be sure. For starters, I was a new teacher, and I was still trying to be a musician and songwriter. Living with a songwriter is pretty tough in itself. At any moment, an idea might pop into my head, and I would have to write it down quickly before it disappeared. Call it compulsive, call it obsessive, call it rude, call it art: whatever it was that made me jump up in the middle of conversation and go into my own world for an hour or so was not easy for Cindi to understand. And I just expected her to understand.

At the time, I was really into Brian Wilson and particularly the mythical *Smile* album which only existed in unfinished bootlegs. Every chance I had, I would read about it, listen to new bootlegs I got in the mail, and re-listen to the old ones. What really struck me as compelling about Brian Wilson was his complete immersion into each track. When he was recording a song about fire, he had all his session musicians wear fire hats and had a barrel with burning wood in the studio. And it really sounded like fire on the track.

I began to take on the immersion philosophy in my writing. I began to completely live the song I was writing. When I wrote about a night on Washington Avenue in Downtown Minneapolis, I went there and sat on the corner all night so I could get the sounds of Washington Avenue into the composition. When I was working on a song about an old clock in an attic, I made a crude wooden "instrument" that recreated the sound of a creaky stairway. I had the bass player hit his string with a mallet because it sounded like the "bong" of an old grandfather clock. As much as I could, I made sure each song personified its subject as completely as possible. It made for good music. Sometimes, it made for really good music.

My eccentric behavior certainly made the guys wonder about me, and pissed off anyone who hung out with me. I would just take off in the middle of any event to write. I was thinking of the music and only the music. Not of anything or anyone else. When we got a good reaction to a song, the guys decided I was justified in my unusual behavior. But Cindi never saw it that way. She saw a self-absorbed punk who was getting off on people's reactions to his own perceived genius. I was just plain hard to live with.

The other problem was, once I began teaching, I spent an excessive amount of time developing the way I graded papers. It was hard for me to go through a paper and not take a long time on it. I also took forever coming up with lesson plans. I was developing everything from scratch. I held myself to the highest standard and was often rewarded for it. While I was learning to teach and continuing to write music, I was ignoring Cindi. I would sit at the computer in the dining room and type, type, type away, not realizing all the while she was in the next room, sad or seething.

To make matters even worse, I would go to rehearsals every Wednesday evening and would gig on the weekends. I'm sure she knew girls were approaching me at the gigs. It wasn't like I was fighting girls off, but I was approached every few gigs and wriggled out of the conversation as quickly as possible. Being shy had its advantages, and I was good at getting myself out of conversations with girls. I had a bit of a natural inclination toward backing off. It was how I was able to stay out of trouble. But Cindi didn't know that. She could make up whatever she wanted about me and other girls I met, and what could I say to convince her otherwise? She had to take my word for it, and that's not easy for someone with trust issues.

And what is obvious to me now is that I was still a kid in many ways. I didn't realize it at the time, but I still thought I was going to make it big. I still was impressed with myself when we got a gig at a big venue or when people approached me on the street and said how much they liked the music. Additionally, I still needed help with grown-up things like taxes. I think Cindi resented my needing that kind of help, and she certainly resented my being so caught up in my own perceived celebrity. I didn't see any of that, but she did. She not only saw it, but she hated it. She resented being with a twenty-five year old. And I had no idea at the time, though it's obvious to me now.

I did realize she was not happy with me, so I did some soul searching. Then I backed off of everything. I'm a people pleaser, so especially since my wife was unhappy with me, I looked inward and decided to do things differently. Instead of writing songs whenever an idea came to me, I just ignored the ideas. That wasn't easy to do because I had had so much luck and attention based on my songwriting ability, but I just told myself I had to grow up and pay attention to my wife instead of my art. It made a lot of sense at the time.

I figured out how to do a less thorough job on student papers and just took lesson plans from other teachers instead of making my own. I wasn't comfortable with either of those changes because I hated to think I wasn't doing as good a job or being as authentic as I wished, but I had to devote more time to Cindi. Period. Everything else had to be downsized.

I stopped gigging as much as possible. I skipped rehearsals. I turned down dates when the drummer called asking if I was available to play. I turned down some pretty prestigious gigs, actually. I pissed off all my band mates quite a few times. They were mad I was saying no, and they were mad I wasn't writing songs anymore. But when I examined what I was doing wrong in Cindi's eyes, music was a huge part of the problem, so I had to slow it way down. I had no choice because the anger in my house was unbearable. And the anger was the result of my own actions.

Since I made so many life changes at once, I began to feel like I was being led down a road I would not normally have chosen to follow. Now I was not only being completely depended upon monetarily, but I was also becoming a bit like a slave who could be treated poorly and still be asked to work hard. You beat the slave down, break his morale, and then tell him to get up and work. That was becoming my role. The reciprocation that Cindi had initially given me in love, life, and communication was quickly fading. In its place were anger and resentment. And I solely and intentionally took the blame. I knew if I completely fessed up to being the problem and changed everything I was doing, there would be nothing more for her to complain about. Boy, was I wrong about that.

The bedroom was her new home. She seldom left it; in bed all day with the TV on. I worked during the day, then came home, made dinner, washed dishes, did laundry, and then began to prepare for the next day's classes as quickly as possible. It was a lonely, unbalanced twist to the relationship and a very unbalanced twist. I was beginning to be unsure what to expect each day. I wondered how much worse things could possible get.

And I was about to get my answer.

Happiness Hidden

The next complaint was the apartment. So we began the search for a house to bring the baby home to. When we finally decided (reluctant as she was because no house really met her approval), I began to pack. I took everything and boxed it and stacked it in the living room of the apartment so that on moving day we would have a very easy move.

Cindi was not happy about the boxes. In addition to my job and the housework, I was packing while she was in bed complaining about the boxes. The boxes! So I ignored her. That was beginning to be the way I dealt, by ignoring, which in itself made her mad, but I had few alternatives. Pacifying Cindi was seldom possible. Getting to the root of any complaint was an act that was completely one-sided. I simply couldn't guess the fix from a one-sided conversation.

It was becoming clear that I had to go it on my own in terms of basic necessities. The house was a good idea, so I made it happen – somewhat with her but mostly in spite of her. I called everyone I knew to help us move. She called no one. My family, friends, band, and college coworkers showed up and took a load or two in their cars. The guys loaded the U-Haul a few times, and in the span of a weekend, we were moved.

Then Cindi was surprisingly happy and began to put things away. Actually living in a house had perked her up.

"See?" I asked her, "What did I tell ya?"

She was glad to be out of the apartment and in a real house. But that wouldn't last long. Houses have problems: leaks, minor fixes waiting to become apparent, basements that sometimes take on water. Soon the young lady who was our realtor and who had become our friend – we hung out with her, her husband, and new baby – finally had enough of Cindi's complaints about the house, and that was that. They stopped returning our calls, and we quit hanging out with them. The former owner got tired of Cindi's calls, too, and finally sent some paperwork restricting her from contacting him. Those two actions themselves really pissed her off.

While all this was happening, we were getting close to baby time. We hired a midwife and began Bradley classes with our doula, Jackie. Jackie was a lot like Cindi. They both had similar childhoods and were able to relate to each other. Jackie was a gorgeous blonde with a very nice boyfriend. She was certified to teach the Bradley method, so every week we went to her house with four other couples who wanted to do natural childbirth: no drugs, no meds, nothing. Just the way cows birthed, according to our hero, Robert A. Bradley.

The weird thing about Jackie was that during the course of our class (and she said this to the whole class), she had gone off the pill and didn't tell her boyfriend. We all knew her little secret, but her poor boyfriend was clueless. It made me kind of sick. Before we were done with our six weeks, she became pregnant. That really made me think. First, she had completely tricked the poor guy, and I felt really bad for him. He had scored this hot girlfriend, but she apparently really only wanted to get pregnant no matter what he thought about it. He seemed to go along with the whole thing when he found out, though, so I was happy about that.

But it also made me wonder if I had been duped like Jackie's boyfriend had. It just put a little seed of doubt in the back of my mind. I guess it isn't that hard for a girl to get pregnant if she wants to. Guys love sex and the feeling of belonging and being mothered. Do that and you can have a baby cooking pretty quickly. It was sad to think about.

To add further complication, Cindi was not happy about my continuing to play with the band. All the extra band stuff I was doing – arranging for other groups, cameo performances, recording with other bands – that all got washed away pretty quickly. Cindi would not have me participate in any of that. With every handful of gigs my band got, I usually had to say no. Another keyboardist, James, was hired to take some of the load off of me and to learn the newer songs that I couldn't be there to pick up. Even rehearsals were becoming hard to get to. When Wednesday night rolled around, there would be a huge fight. I often conceded and called the guys to cancel. James was there and could learn the new material, so I wasn't worried about the band. But my days in the group were numbered.

Luckily, before things had gotten really bad, I had been able to lay down all my organ and vocal parts for the new album. I desperately wanted to be there to help mix down the tracks that I had written, but I only got out of the house once to be able to do some of it. I was able to make a few corrections, but there is still stuff on the album that I wished I could have fixed before it went to pressing. Still, I thought the other guys did a great job without me.

Cindi just made such a big deal about my spending time on music that I couldn't live with her *and* pull my weight in the band. Some of the guys understood, but they were becoming concerned for me. I tried to tell them not to worry. Others were angry because I was letting the band down. It felt awful and incredibly lonely.

We began scheduling fewer and fewer gigs. I just couldn't do very many because it meant having to walk into the house at two in the morning only to deal with the repercussions of having been gone that night. There was so much anger, so much resentment. It took a week to get Cindi off the topic. She hated the band, hated the time I spent on my music, as much as I had cut it down. She had refused to go to any gigs ever since I had "ignored" her at the Uptown bar. At least I didn't have to deal with her during my gigs, but the guys had hurt feelings too, because I wasn't pulling my weight. It seemed that no matter what I did or where I went, I was letting someone down. I couldn't win.

One night, we had a gig at the Turf Club in St. Paul. While we were meeting the opening band, I saw a face I had not seen in a long time: Elizabeth. We had gone out before Cindi, but I had scared her off by bringing her flowers. There she was, a year and a half later at the Turf Club, and she looked better than ever. Elizabeth looked like happiness embodied. I can't say it any better than that. She reminded me of a far less complicated time. Her dark, curly hair and sexy eyes were the first things I saw. She was unmistakable. She looked like the cutest little German girl all grown up and gorgeous. Her sideways smile grew as her eyes met mine.

"John, I was hoping you would be here. You're still playing with the band!"

"Liz." I hugged her. She smelled sweet and lemony as I put my face to her hair. "You smell great."

She laughed. "It's the way I always smell, John." We let go and she stared at me intently, continuing to touch my arm. Her eyes sparkled. I couldn't stop staring at her beautifully dark curls, sweet smile, and gorgeous curvy hips; it was so nice to see her. "You haven't had many gigs lately."

"No." I grew silent.

"John, what's wrong?"

Then I just spilled everything. It was like I couldn't stop; the story just kept coming.

I told her about everything: the baby, the marriage, the new house, the constant anxiety of being with Cindi. Elizabeth said she felt terrible for me. She wanted to help. She wanted to come up with solutions to help me and Cindi. Elizabeth understood both sides. She felt so bad for us. We talked for a bit, and then it was time for the first band to start and for the other band, us, to warm up downstairs. I told her I would be back up in a bit.

We all grabbed new beers and a few other items and headed over the chain at the top of the basement stairs to the dimly lit, vacant Clown Lounge Bar, closed for our show. We did our vocal warm-ups, drank our beers, passed around a joint, and listened to the band upstairs. They were pretty good, and we were becoming loose. No more Cindi, no more horror for the night until after the sweeping joy of the music had abated. We joked, smoked, horsed around, walked on the bar, and looked in the back room for old bar junk to steal: harmless fun the band was used to at all the bars in the Twin Cities. We planned our big entrance and then went back upstairs.

Elizabeth was sitting at a booth by herself watching the band, so I went and sat down next to her. "What were you guys up to down there?" She wondered.

"We usually warm up before the show. How about you?"

"You sound happier!" she observed.

"Yeah, this is going to be fun! We have some special plans for the show. You'll have to wait and see."

"I want to talk to you after, ok?"

"Yeah. You gonna be here that late?"

"Of course. I came here to see you. And I have a few ideas for you and your situation."

"Ok, great. This is turning out to be a good night." My stomach suddenly, momentarily, tightened. "It's gonna be hell when I get home, but I don't care about that right now!"

"Good," Liz said. She scooted over, closer to me in the booth and put her hand on my leg. The affection, such a small movement and touch, was unbelievably calming. I sat back in the booth, and she put her head on my shoulder. I was in heaven for a very calm, serene moment. I had no idea how terribly I had missed such affection, little as it was.

After the show, I walked Liz to her car. She held my hand. I was scared to reciprocate, knowing this action was over the line, but I allowed it anyway. I knew I should be home with my wife, somehow helping her, working for her, but I could not get this kind of attention there. Only anger. Only the cold shoulder. Only what I should have done or should be doing. But at that moment, on the way to Elizabeth's car, her hand took me to a place that was simply pure love. She led me along without anger, without repercussion, without asking anything in return except that I feel better.

She unlocked her door, turned, and leaned back against it. Then she grabbed my forearm and pulled gently. She peered into my eyes and guided my head down toward hers while gently caressing my ear. I had such hesitation. She knew I did.

She said, "It's ok."

I melted against her, and our lips met. All my sadness was temporarily erased. In its place: happiness, pure happiness. We stood pressed together for about ten minutes. Then I broke it off.

I had to go. Had to face what I knew was coming. Had to go back and endure the anger, the yelling. Had to go back and admit to myself how awful I was. How much more terrible I was now becoming because I had allowed that kiss to occur on top of all my other missteps that Cindi could list as easily as reciting her address and phone number. I had to live with being all the bad things she called me, and now, secretly, with being the guy who cheated on her.

Liz had smelled so good. Her perfume was on my face. I showered, stashed my smoky, perfumed clothes in the washer, and started it up. I was now hiding something; that was for sure. I went back upstairs and lay down in bed. Cindi was turned away from me – her usual position in bed and in general. I turned away as well and thought of Elizabeth as I dozed off. In the middle of hell, I mused, I could at least remember my moment of heaven, hidden but where I could still almost touch it.

Time to Transition

Most times the band played after that, Liz came to see us. We never got overly physical; never had sex. But I could come up to her before the show, put my hand in her back pocket, talk quietly to her, and she would know I would walk her to her car after the show. The guys gave me looks sometimes, but most of them either understood or had similar relationships going on.

Elizabeth didn't really want anything from me. That was clear, and I was happy about that. I just loved to climb in the car with her after a gig, the two of us still a little sweaty from the bar, and pretzel ourselves in her front seat, kissing affectionately. From her perspective, I was taken and therefore no longer a threat. From mine, hers was the only real love I received. It was only physical, not at all emotional, but it was enough for the time being. I knew there would be no way we could ever be a couple. She was way too jumpy about the subject and made sure I understood her intentions were purely physical. She didn't have a boyfriend and didn't want one. She had her own issues.

We came close to having sex only once, but we both knew we would never really get there. Her sexy hips, thighs, and butt felt so great, tightly pressed against me, slowly grinding in my lap. That never happened to me at home. Elizabeth's beautiful face and lips, ever-longing for mine, were so comfortable. Other than her hot body, there wasn't much more to her from my perspective. You would think we would have been madly making love, but it just wasn't like that. She was empty. She was becoming addicted to pain killers, and they made her increasingly vacant. Quite frankly, I was scared to death to have sex with a chick I didn't really like. That hadn't worked out well previously. To be in an equivalent position with another flaky chick would have been very bad. I was disgusted by the thought of having sex with someone who couldn't reciprocate. The lack of a real relationship was probably for the better from my point of view. I didn't need another lingering complication.

One night after a gig at the Uptown, I walked Elizabeth to her car for the last time. We had become complacent with the arrangement, losing interest in the non-relationship featuring only snipped moments of affection. We had quickly become bored with each other, yet neither of us wanted more out of the relationship than just what we were doing. Elizabeth had her own problems to work through with the pain killers and alcohol, and therefore she became more and more unapproachable as time went on. I kissed her for a minute outside her car, and then she drove away. I remembered thinking she would turn out more or less like Cindi in a relationship. That was a sad, lonely thought. I walked to my car and drove home. I was very much alone again.

In terms of this relationship, there was no good and bad. There were no extremes. I felt good to have the physical proximity of a beautiful girl who wasn't yelling at me or cursing my existence. I felt bad that I had eventually, despite my ability to play girls off, selfishly given into my own emotional needs. The extremes were not two ends of a spectrum, however. They were just confusingly mixed together.

You fight to stay in a relationship. That's what I was taught by my parents. You fight for the marriage. But with Liz, I wasn't fighting for Cindi. I was on a beautiful oasis away from her. I thoroughly enjoyed the lack of her presence during those stolen moments. It was wonderful, and it was also contrary to everything I believed should be a part of a marriage. I was neither happy nor sad about it, yet I was both. I regretted it, and I also knew it allowed me to bear the relationship a little longer. It was odd to not be in a situation that I perceived as all good or all bad. I could actually see them simultaneously. At any rate, being able to hang in there, as it turned out, was a good thing since we had a baby on the way.

In fact, when I got home from my last meeting with Liz, Cindi was on the floor in the bathroom washing out the tub. She had just thrown up all over the bathtub. Not only that, her water had just broken. She was angry I had taken so long to get home but did not have the energy or the attention to yell much. The contractions had kept her mind off of how much she hated me.

I got her on the phone with the nurse line, and they timed her contractions. They were over an hour apart. It was time to get our things together, but not quite time to leave, provided the contractions didn't suddenly speed up. We could probably wait until morning. She called Jackie, and they agreed on six A.M. to meet at our house and drive to the hospital together. That gave me about five hours to sleep.

When I woke up, Cindi was packed and ready to go. I got dressed and was downstairs in time to meet Jackie at the door. She asked Cindi all her doula questions, went through last minute stuff, and then we were off to the hospital. It was time to do it like cows do!

We got settled in our room and plugged in the CD player. I suppose cows don't use CD players, but it was still allowed. The hospital was a hospital. What I mean by that is it looked and felt like a hospital and not so much like a place cows would give birth. Beige tiles, white walls, hard surfaces, countertops, and the oddly-shaped tables on wheels. We had seen some video in class of home births in a huge rented tub, and although the tub looked to be a little much for someone's living room, it was still more comfortable looking. This room was unlike the living room in the video. It was cold and hard. You couldn't just sit on the floor. But it would have to do.

I was prepared with our doula to watch for the stages of childbirth and do what was necessary during each one. We propped pillows on the uncomfortable bed. We drew a bath in the bathtub with silver handles everywhere. We turned this way and that. I held Cindi's hand. It wasn't long before she was completely naked (which isn't unusual) and trying everything she could to get comfortable through the contractions. Nothing was working. The pain began to be unbearable.

The midwife finally put a monitor on the baby's head, and he (yes, he) was in some distress with each contraction. She felt Cindi's stomach and said it seemed that the baby was sideways. His head was not down, it was to the side. Something had to be done to get him into the right position. The pain was increasing. We had to begin to think of some ways to intervene…to interfere with Bradley's perfect vision of natural childbirth. It had been about 18 hours since we had arrived at the hospital.

Jackie, the strongest supporter of natural childbirth, looked at me as I asked, "Do you think we should try an epidural?" The nurse had said it would help.

"I think we'd better," she said. I was surprised. "This is not normal," she said with a look of fear. It was somewhat alarming and also comforting to hear that from her. Cindi was in such pain, and the baby was in trouble. We walked over to Cindi and told her what we thought. She quickly agreed to the epidural.

Unfortunately, the epidural itself was not quick to come. It took over an hour for the team to get to our room. She was in terrible pain and nothing helped. By the time they got there, the baby was in real trouble. His heart rate went way down with each contraction. The good news was the epidural worked quickly. Before we knew it, things were loosening up, and the baby was facing down. Everyone breathed a sigh of relief.

When Charles first came out, they washed him off, weighed, and measured him. Then they tried to get him to nurse but with no luck. He began to fall asleep. So the nurses uncovered him to make him cold, so he would wake up and at least try a few sucks. Then, within about a minute, he turned a deep purple.

Everything happened at once. The nurses wrapped him up, grabbed him away from Cindi, put him on one of the little rolling baby beds, and ran out the door with him.

I called, "Don't worry," to Cindi and ran down the hall after the rolling, purple baby. I thought, "Luckily we're in a hospital!"

We ended up in a room with zillions of warming lights. It was a little like a greenhouse but with crying. The nurse took off Charles's blanket and lowered the heat lamp down over him. I put my finger in his hand, and he grabbed on the way little babies do. Then I told him all about the delivery, how he had gotten stuck, how he had gotten too cold, so here we were in the warm-up room. Finally, he turned pink again and drifted off to sleep. I went back to Cindi to report that he was doing better.

When we went home the next day, Cindi's mom came for a week to help out. This was when I learned that Cindi and her mom were like two ends of a set of jumper cables already attached to a live battery. Touching them together too much meant things would become explosive. By the end of the week, they got into a hair-pulling match, and her mom immediately returned to Colorado.

Next, it was time for colic. It felt like Charles cried non-stop for the next week. One night, trying to think of ideas for positions he might like, I put him on my forearm facing down, his chin between my thumb and forefinger, his butt up by my bicep. Suddenly, the crying stopped. So that was my role every night with Charles: face down, butt up, walking the floor, singing quietly while Cindi slept.

Unfortunately, it wasn't long before my semester break was up, and I had to go back and start classes. This meant that Cindi would be on her own with Charles for the first time. What I didn't know was that Cindi's disposition, the one I had come to know and hate, was only a teaser. Postpartum depression, on top of what already existed, was about to take me from the tame problems I had already experienced to the real show.

From the Abyss   John Emil Augustine

For Worse

I remember the first few weeks went ok after I went back to work. But as the initial Cindi-Charles alone time increased, things began to get a little scary. I usually wasn't sure what to think when I got home at night.

The first thing I remember was that Cindi ended up holding Charles all day, every day. Everything she did was with Charles on her arm or in a sling. When she put him down, he cried. That was not a good thing. It made her angry. I understand the feeling because too much crying can make just about anyone lose it eventually. Then again, when you put the child down at appropriate times while he is crying, he learns to self-soothe. It is an important skill for later in life.

Anyway, the constant holding, though not as grating as constant crying, was wearing on Cindi's nerves, nonetheless. I remember walking in the door one evening and having Charles shoved into my arms. Then I watched Cindi begin to scream at the top of her lungs and run upstairs to the bedroom. This I had not seen before. I was perplexed and a little worried for Charles's safety. What was going on?

All I heard were muffled screams from upstairs for a half hour. I tried to be calm and get Charles some formula from the pantry and mix it according to the directions. No microwaving! I was looking very carefully at the sticker on the formula bottle, my body shaking ever-so-slightly as I held Charles. I wanted him to experience calm and regularity even while his mom's strange behavior was occurring above our heads. I wanted to send him the message, "No problem. We're cool." It was, at best, a mixed message.

He wasn't hungry, so I kept up my vigil with him until Cindi finally came downstairs. She was overwhelmed by caring for a baby, she said. Then she left. She just took off walking. So I put Charles in the stroller and followed her.

We ended up on our regular route around the lake. Charles slept. It was May, and the warm spring air was becoming fragrant.

From the Abyss   John Emil Augustine

The evening was brilliantly vivid to me as I took in the bright greens and blues, and the sweet smell of the spring air.

"God, everything seems hazy," Cindi said as we walked. "I feel like my brain is in a cloud."

"Really?"

"It's like everything is confusing and…I don't know. Ah!"

I thought about it as we walked. "Baby blues?" I finally asked.

"What?"

"You know, postpartum depression."

"I don't know. Maybe."

I suddenly felt awful for her. Here I had been feeling bad for myself because I had to deal with her. What an idiot, I thought.

She agreed to see a doctor. We got some happy pills for her, and they worked for a while. They worked well, actually. After a few months, she decided that since she was feeling so good, she didn't need them anymore.

I said, "Hey, if you don't want to take them, then don't." What did I know?

Then things were fine for a few more months. But the effects of the pills began to wear off. When I was home, Cindi became belligerent and mean. She watched Charles, and I did the housework and my job. I put in my eight hour day at school, then dove into my schoolwork at home. Then housework. Things were becoming too far out of balance. Cindi resented me and made sure I knew it.

I had two options: dutifully take orders or be more awful than she was. Doing the latter meant I would probably go too far. I had to be careful, or I could end up in jail. Again, no one is concerned with the dad's feelings. But when the dad acts on his feelings, he is at fault. And guys tend to act with physical violence. It must be the testosterone. I had to avoid getting to that point.

So I walked the fine line. I stayed calm the best I could and took it. When Cindi said she wanted a divorce, I told her I would not divorce her. When pressed, she couldn't tell me what I was doing that was horrible enough to warrant a divorce. Still, she kept asking. She knew it hurt my feelings. I was trying to make this work, single-handedly! She could have at least acknowledged my one-sided contribution, I thought. Asking for a divorce was the opposite of an appropriate reaction to my efforts.

I was miserable. There is a picture from that summer that I eventually turned into an album cover. Cindi wanted to take pictures of her garden in the backyard on a role of black and white film one day. It was one of those hot summer days during which we had fought the heat as well as each other all morning. For some reason, in the afternoon, Cindi was feeling better and wanted to use up her film. The last picture was of me and Charles. She kept asking me to smile, but I just didn't have it in me. I couldn't smile any more than I could make clouds cover the squelching sun. Later, I would ask for that picture because it was the only one of me and Charles from that time. We both look gray in the picture, like all happiness had long since dropped out of us.

Every day I drove home from work, they began: the panic attacks that were coming on more frequently. The closer I got to our house, the faster my heart raced. What would it be like today? Would Cindi be calm? Would the house be a disaster? Would I have to find a way to come up with dinner, or would she have something ready? Would we have an all-night fight about getting a divorce? I just never knew what I was about to walk into.

No matter what I did, I felt guilty. Of course I felt guilty about Elizabeth even though the relationship had ended. I would always be the guy who had cheated on his wife. More than that, I felt guilty about everything that was currently happening. I felt guilty about sticking Cindi with the baby during the day. I felt guilty for working long hours. I felt guilty for being in a band. I felt guilty for writing music or practicing parts I needed to learn when I was at home. I felt guilty for spending time grading papers or working on lesson plans. I felt guilty because I could not fix something in the house or would fix it but would do a poor job at it. I even felt guilty about fixing anything because I was home but not attending to Cindi and the baby or to my own work. I felt guilty when Cindi mowed the lawn with the baby in tow when I was at work. I felt guilty when I mowed the lawn because I was leaving Cindi alone with the baby. I felt guilty I could not rekindle our relationship, and I felt guilty about how much I hated the thought of rekindling our relationship. Guilt engulfed and swallowed me.

Eventually, I began trying to lie my way out of the holes I fell into. Always on defense, I tried to just say whatever it was I thought Cindi wanted to hear. Unfortunately, at least half the time I was wrong about what she wanted to hear, and then I would try unsuccessfully to switch my position. I no longer knew what to do. I couldn't appease her, couldn't tell her what I thought she wanted to hear, certainly couldn't tell her the truth that I was just trying to tip-toe around her to stay out of fights. I just ended up being a punching bag who was now a liar on top of everything else. In trying to do what I had perceived to be the right thing, I ended up doing more and more wrong things. I was becoming someone I didn't even know. The only problem was I didn't know whether I was acting out of character or not. That question really ate at me.

We are supposed to be held accountable for our actions, and that was exactly my plan. Everything I did and anything that happened to us as a family, I took personal responsibility for. What I did wrong and what Cindi did wrong: these were my fault. I set out to correct every problem. But in Cindi's eyes, not only was every misstep a big deal, but my corrections were never good enough either, and therefore became a big deal as well.

The house and my job were great examples. I had found us a house because she hated the apartment. But the house wasn't good enough. Stupidly, I tried to point out the bright side, but that just fueled the fire. So I would try to fix things, but I did poorly in her opinion, and that fueled the fire as well. In terms of my job, I had a shitty job in landscaping, so I found a teaching gig. Unfortunately, I could not control my schedule and would have to teach night classes which angered Cindi to no end. So I worked it out with the school that they would schedule only one night class per semester no matter what, but that wasn't good enough for her either. I held myself accountable for every shortcoming, deserved or not. Someone had to be blamed for all the problems Cindi saw, so I took the blame voluntarily.

However, being held accountable for our problems and my shortcomings wasn't good enough. So I eventually side-stepped issues she would bring up which, of course, made me look bad. Why was I changing the subject? Why was I lying? When I assumed accountability for anything, I was ridiculed. When I shifted the accountability to someone or something else, I was ridiculed and called a liar. There was no way to avoid Cindi's intense anger. I was stuck, and anything I did made matters worse. Accountable or not, I was the bad guy. Whether I really was or not, I turned into a deplorable human being in Cindi's eyes, and she was the only person who mattered to me. I believed her every criticism of me, and I subsequently questioned every move I made over and over again.

I developed ticks: unusual compulsive movements. I didn't notice them until Cindi pointed them out. Yet another thing that I was doing wrong. Ticks and panic attacks were the result of all the stress that had built up and from which I could never hide, day or night. I still have them today, ticks and attacks. These are the permanent scars that always remind of where I was and how bad it became. It was a time during which I felt bad about everything I did; I was the bad guy, always. It was a downward, quickening spiral.

What did I do that was so bad? What am I leaving out of this story to make myself look good? When I look back at it now, having done some pretty bad stuff since, I actually can't point to one thing and say, "This is what made me so hard to live with." I was a kid and could be a real smart ass. Neither of those things endeared me. I was obsessive over my job and my music and could get very absorbed in either. That was annoying. I went behind Cindi's back and tried to do what I believed to be the right things despite her objections. She understandably hated that. And I cheated on her with Elisabeth, though she never knew. That was the worst. Everything else, her anger, her hatred, and her manipulative behavior were the result of her mental illness. What that illness is I have never learned, though I have my hypotheses. I have certainly learned that it doesn't go away and that most people are quick to judge me and not believe me about the way she is. So be it. Judge away. But now, as I write these words, there is no doubt in my mind that I did the best I could in the situation. That isn't saying much, but it is the truth. I acted well, I acted poorly, and I am sure somebody more adept than I could have done better. I simply know that I did the best *I* could at that point in my life though I am ashamed I did not do better.

From the Abyss John Emil Augustine

Knowing I did my best doesn't make me feel better about any of it. It is just something I now know about myself. I have no desire to falsely make myself look good, because I am neither good nor bad; I am human and have accepted myself as such. In fact, I am going to write about plenty of terrible things I have done. Being in an abusive relationship is not one of them.

If you are in an abusive relationship, know that you, too, are human. Accept that you have done the best you could, and then get the hell out of the situation any way you can. I know it's not easy. God, how I know it's not easy, but you can do it. Get out. Period.

At night in bed, I would think back to long before that summer of 2001. I had just started college. It was January 1993. My grandpa taught at the college I attended and had given me a copy of his office key, so I could study there when he was in class. Once in a while our breaks overlapped, and he would end up telling me about the old days.

His mom had been tough to live with. Sometimes she would have her and my grandpa's stuff packed when he got home from school, and they would leave. His dad, a very stable, thoughtful guy, would come home to an empty house and not know what was going on. He would call around town to friends and relatives until he found them and convince her to come back.

Leaving like that happened throughout my grandpa's childhood, right through young adulthood, and into his mid-30s when his dad finally died. He told me as an adult, he would sometimes get a call from his mother in the middle of the night, screaming, crying, and telling him his dad was cheating on her. He would have to leave while his wife and children slept and make the long drive from Minneapolis to Lacrosse to try to resolve the situation himself. Often his dad had his checkbook out, telling her to do the math: there was no way he could have been out with someone else and have the same balance in the checkbook.

My grandpa said he had asked his dad over and over, "Pa, why don't you just leave her?"

His dad would always reply, "Son, I married her for better or for worse. For better or for worse." Twice said to underscore the importance of the agreement he had made. My grandpa said he never understood the point of going through the same horrid game again and again.

I saw the wisdom in my great-grandpa's tenacious and steadfast commitment, and I decided to tough this out for Charles. Still, I wondered if I was beginning to feel how my great-grandfather had felt from the 1930s through the 1960s. Every night, according to my grandpa, he had taken two Bromo-Seltzer tablets for his upset stomach. By 1960, he had developed a stomach problem that killed him that same year.

The upset stomach, I understood that. It was stress, and I was feeling it myself, every night when I got home. If my great-grandmother was anything like Cindi, and I stuck it out, then what? What kind of life was this turning out to be? Was this what marriage was like for people? Are we all relegated to the promises we made before we knew what we were actually promising?

But I did know. I knew what I was getting myself into. I couldn't pretend I was unaware. I had made my decision. Now I had to stand by my word. I had to do this for Charles's sake. I had to be the stabilizer. What would have become of my grandpa had he not had his dad's unmoving stability? All his uncles on his mother's side were drunks. The family was a menagerie of homeless, hopeless, and helpless degenerates. His dad had toughed it out for him.

Though I was toughing it out, I knew I was getting into a tough fix. Every night I would stumble through these thoughts. What was the answer? What was to happen? This was up to me. How would I handle myself? How would I make the situation bearable? How would I help my son? How would I not snap Cindi's neck?

Then something occurred to me – just a thought in the back of my head. My great-grandma was alive and had not seen the baby by his three month mark. She was the only family member who had not met him.

I thought about her – how I hated to talk to her. I hated to be at her place or to be on the phone with her. The first ten minutes or so would be nice, and then she would start in. They stole her husband's Bible when she was moved. Her son stole all her money. They locked her in this room and never saw her. The whole apartment complex hated her. If I could just take her somewhere, she would buy us a night out, and it would be like when I was a kid. You couldn't help but feel guilty after an hour with her.

Even so, as bad as she had gotten, her family had been there for her and cared for her as best as we could, especially my grandpa, her son. And she hated him. Loathed him. He had taken her house when she became unable to walk. He had moved her to Minneapolis and imprisoned her. Still, he dutifully visited her, helped her, made her furniture, and fixed things for her. For better or for worse.

All this I mulled over and decided to tell Cindi I needed to take Charles to see his great grandmother. I didn't tell her I felt as though I needed to learn something from my great-grandma, nor did I tell her that I expected to garner some bit of wisdom to use for my relationship with Cindi from our visit. And maybe it was a symbolic knowledge; a symbolic visit. I didn't know. I just knew I had to go. It was, after all, only across town.

Cindi agreed to the visit.

At first.

Perhaps Answers

Cindi agreed to the visit, but the morning of the visit came, and Cindi decided she couldn't go. So I said I would take Charles myself, but she decided Charles could not go either. He had had a hard night, and she didn't want him to leave the house. So I called my great-grandma and canceled. But I made a second date for about two weeks from then. It was my sneaky way of getting over there despite Cindi. "This isn't going to go away!" I was telling her.

I really thought I was going to learn something from the visit: some connection, some piece of the puzzle. Why was all this happening? Was I meant to stay in this relationship? Would it get better? I didn't realize it then, but in my quest to better understand it, I was moving farther away from the relationship itself. By solely trying to solve our problems, I was working against the very nature of a relationship. But I was out of ideas and didn't have a partner who would help.

Two weeks later, Cindi consented to the visit, and we went to the nursing home. There were my great-grandma's things: furniture, magazines, and ketchup and mustard packets she had been saving from the cafeteria. The packets were everywhere. She found a bag, put them all in it, and handed it to me. She supposed that with a baby we would need some help, and she could at least give us some free condiments. It was always interesting to me how nice and mean she could be all in the same visit.

After the first ten minutes, she got on with slamming my grandpa. She went on and on about the things he stole, how poorly he treated her, how he had illegitimate children in Hawaii. Who knew what truths were hidden in the accusations? Although she was in her 90s, she seemed completely lucid yet was completely a con artist at the same time. Sorting truth from fiction was impossible. She could convince anybody of anything; she had the nurses at the home confront my grandpa a number of times about where her money and possessions were.

He would patiently answer their questions, though it was no business of theirs. He would show bank statements, tell exactly where each item in question was, and tell the dimensions of the furniture she was requesting and explain that some things just wouldn't fit in her tiny room. She had the nurses so convinced of how terribly treated she was by my grandpa that he would walk in prepared with facts and evidence.

She fed us the same stories that day, not knowing I had been in on the decisions such as what would fit in the room, what was most important for her to have, where the family Bible was (which I pulled out and showed her), and where her money was. It was carefully saved and allocated to the nursing home. Extra money had been set aside for anything else she asked for, provided it was a reasonable item like a TV or her own silverware. The nursing home provided some of the things she wanted: magazine subscriptions and food. The infomercials she saw in the middle of the night with miracle laundry detergent or insoles, sadly, she could not order. Things like that were simply not necessary. I felt bad telling her she could not do or have certain things, but the reality was she had to save her money for her own well-being. After all, who knew how long she would live! Try telling all that to a crabby old lady who could masquerade as a sweet old lady and who was used to getting her way any way she could.

Somewhere, taken on that same roll of black and white film, is a picture of Charles with his great-great-grandma. He is screaming, and she is trying her best to balance him in her scrawny arms. When we left, I had learned nothing. She was as awful as ever, and I was no closer to finding my way in my relationship with Cindi.

The strange thing was that two days later, my great-grandma died. That night, shortly before she died, my mom called and asked for help. My great-grandma was too weak to walk more than ten steps. Still, she was determined not to die in her chair, so she would take off down the hall and fall. Then she had to be carried back. They needed back-up, so I went right away.

By time I got there, my great-grandma had calmed down some. She had pneumonia. They had her on antibiotics, but since pneumonia is a virus, the antibiotics weren't really helping. Her lungs were filling with fluid. Her body was too weak to fight the virus. She was conscious and fighting to leave the building when I got there but was not like that for long. After a few hours, she was unconscious and her breathing began to have a gurgle. I guess they call that the death rattle. She was going to die in her chair.

So we propped her up with pillows and gave her water with a sponge on a little blue hospital straw. She could still suck the water out of the little sponge. But she wouldn't be able to do even that for long. She was becoming less and less aware. She was literally drowning. The nurse called me, my mom, and grandma out into the hall. It was not looking like she was going to get better. Her body could not fight the pneumonia. They could at least make her more comfortable by giving her morphine. It may not cure her, the nurse said. In fact, it might make her worse. Still, she wouldn't feel any pain, so we agreed to it.

I remember going home before she died, leaving my grandma there with my great-grandma alone. She was out cold, and her breaths were becoming shorter, shallower. The rattle was becoming more pronounced as more fluid built up in her lungs. Her fingers, from the tips and moving slowly down to the hands, were turning purple. It wouldn't be long. Still, I knew I had to get home because Cindi was going to be pissed I was out so late. It wouldn't matter why. She would have been up with Charles and would be irate. So I left my grandma there alone waiting for the rattle to stop.

On my way home, I remember thinking how much alike the processes of birth and death were. There wasn't much anyone could do except try to keep the person who was in pain comfortable. The epidural and the morphine helped. But the inevitable would happen regardless: the baby would come out, and the life would go out. That connection didn't help me out of my predicament, didn't answer any questions I was seeking answers to, but it did give me something else to think about.

After all, what had my great-grandma's life been for? Why had she been alive? No one liked her...well, not for very long anyway. When she died, everyone was relieved. No more awful talks with her. No more guilt trips. What benefit did she have to the planet in her ninety-some years? That was a tough question to answer. It can be difficult to figure out what good some people have done while alive.

Perhaps my grandpa was the one good thing. People loved him. He helped people. Of course! My great-grandmother was unimportant, as was Cindi. Charles was the point of all this. He could do what Cindi couldn't: lead a life to benefit, not hurt, others. At least I could try to help him with this.

But Charles couldn't be separated from Cindi. This was a complex puzzle. How could I pull this off? Would Charles even want to lead a good life? Would he be able to differentiate? Perhaps I could give him my example. My great-grandfather had given my grandpa a good example to follow. My grandpa got the idea. I could do this for Charles.

But was I really qualified to be a good example to Charles? From Cindi's perspective, I was awful. What if she was right? It was possible that I would try to be a good example only to have my effort backfire on me. The way I had been raised, the way I thought and reacted to things, perhaps they were completely wrong. That really was Cindi's opinion. It was hard to say who was better suited to be a good role model. She wanted me out of the picture, and maybe she was right.

Still, I thought, even if I was one type of role model and Cindi was another, Charles should have the choice. He should be able to experience both of us and decide how he wanted to act when he grew up. Maybe he would be a hybrid of Cindi's and my way of operating. I had to at least expose him to each way of doing things.

When I got home, it was past midnight. Cindi was up with Charles, walking as I usually did with him. He was crying, and she was fuming. But she hadn't hurt him. She handed him to me as a quarterback would plant a football between the arms of a running back.

"What were you doing!" she shouted.

"My great-grandma is dying."

"What did they need you for?"

"She wouldn't stay in her chair, and then she would fall in the hall, and we would have to carry her back. They were trying to keep her in her room."

"So you held her down?"

"No. I carried her back."

"You know what, forget it! You and your whole family are so sick. I can't believe I am still here!"

"What?"

"I can't believe I am still here!" She screamed. Charles cried and twisted in my arms as I moved this way and that to hold onto him. I had nothing to say to that.

Cindi went to the kitchen, twisted her feet into her sandals, and opened the door. *"From now on, you're on your own!"* She screamed.

I stood there with a crying baby and watched her open and slam the door. I moved to the kitchen window, only to see her run through the backyard.

Where was she going?

She opened the gate, went into the driveway, quickly got into the car, backed away from the garage, and screamed out of the driveway.

As I stood watching, I had set Charles onto the counter and against my chest as he cried. I picked him up, sat down on the kitchen floor, vexed, and held him up near my face. "Hey, little boy," I half-whispered, "You're ok. Hey, Charlie, no worries. What you wanna do? You tired? Hungry? I suppose you're going to need something to eat, huh bud?" He calmed a bit when he heard the sound of my voice. Those big baby-sobs started to come as he reversed his own crying. "Well, what do ya say? Should we get some food? At least we can try to eat something; and if you don't want to do that, you can sleep, huh?"

I slowly got up and held him close, all the time looking at him and talking quietly. "I know, Charlie, I know. It's tough all over, isn't it? Well, we won't let that get us down. Nope, not us. We're gonna be just fine." He began to close his eyes. He was tired, the poor guy. I laid him down in my left arm. "There ya go. You sleep a little, and I'll see what I can do, ok? Yeah, you're tired, huh? Just have a little break there, guy. Now we're cookin'. Now we're cookin'."

He was falling asleep, and I was shaking uncontrollably.

From the Abyss   John Emil Augustine

Crazy

We were out of formula, so at two in the morning I went to the Rainbow Foods on Snelling and University to buy baby formula. There I was in the store with a sleeping baby in my arms, trying to remember what Jackie the doula had said was the best kind. I took my best stab at it, went through the checkout, and loaded Charles back into my truck under the lights of the grocery store parking lot. "This is crazy," I thought. The air was cooling.

When I got home, I saw that Cindi's car was back, but there were also two squad cars with flashing lights in front of our house. "Now what?" I thought.

I walked in the back door ready for anything. Cindi had come home, found us gone, and called the cops on me. She took Charles as I walked through the door, and then she identified me to the officer. She bounced and rocked the baby, saying, "There, there. There, there. Shhh, shhhh, shhh."

I tried to explain that I was at the store buying formula, but she insisted she had been home and said I had taken the baby from her. I tried to describe the situation as it had happened, but cops tend to believe the mother. When I showed them the baby formula in the grocery bag, they finally told me that if I left the premises there would not be trouble. If Cindi wanted, she could file for a restraining order against me.

So I drove to across the river to Minneapolis at about three in the morning and camped out in Roland's laundry room for the rest of the night. I let myself in and slept on the cement floor in a sleeping bag I found. When I woke up, there was Roland with a basket full of laundry.

"Dude…what are you doing here? You get kicked out?" The sunlight came through the little basement window, spilling in around the blue curtain made from a bed sheet.

So I told him what had happened. He said, as only Roland can, "Dude, that really sucks. What are you going to do?"

"I don't know." I stared at the wall. I suddenly realized I really had no way to conjure a plan at the moment.

"Well, you can stay here if you need to. We actually have a spare bedroom upstairs."

"Let me call home first. Maybe this will blow over."

"Dude, seriously, is everything all right?"

"For the most part, yes. Thanks."

"Ok. Just let me know."

So I called my house. "Are we done with this?"

"I don't know, John. That is up to you."

"Ok, we're done. I'm coming home. You going to call the cops on me?"

"No."

"Ok. See you in a bit."

So I drove back to St. Paul. No cops waited outside my house. I let myself in and sat down at the kitchen table with some toast and coffee. Cindi held Charles and watched me.

"From now on," I blurted with food in my mouth, "no more Mr. Nice Guy, Cindi. You want to call the cops on me; I will give you a real reason to call the cops. You want to be mean, I will be mean. Don't question it; just know I can be as mean as you. You want me in jail, I will be sure to take you down with me. You act nice, I act nice. You act like a bitch, I will out-bitch, out-asshole, out-muscle you any day. You want that, you keep this up." She was silent, but glared intently as she quickly rocked back and forth with the baby. "But just remember, you are about to lose your sole source of income. You come after me for money while I am in jail and see what happens. Good luck! So you think long and hard about how much you want to hurt me, and then just remember: that equates to how much you are going to hurt yourself. Go ahead, if it makes you feel good, and try me. You're gonna be in for an awful lotta hurt."

As she stood there, her rocking had picked up speed. I was on my second piece of toast; the chunks I spit during my speech were on the table in front of me. I didn't care. I was about to throw down if she wanted to fuck with me.

"So this is you threatening me?"

I tried to stay calm. "This is me saying equal force. Equal force. You want to fight? I haven't even started to fight. Now I'm telling you, you will get equal the amount you can put out. No more, no less."

"So you're threatening me."

"I am telling you if you play nice, I play nice. You play mean, I play mean. That makes it your choice. So, no, I am not threatening you. I am telling you that you are threatening yourself. You create the threat, and I will turn it back on you. If that threatens you, it's your problem."

"Ok...? That seems like a threat."

"Call the cops then. Tell them that I said if you act mean, I will act mean right back. See what they say. They take me away, and there goes your income. Everything will be equal. Be nice, and I will be nice."

Silence.

"Go ahead, pick up the phone. I'll dial if you want. I will say my wife is threatened by me because I am not backing down. Let them come. I go; you go...one way or the other."

She went into the living room, and I swear to God I assumed she would call the cops. I even took off the hemp necklace my buddy made me and stashed it in a drawer, so it wouldn't get taken while I was in jail.

For a few minutes, silence. Nothing. Charles was playing quietly on the floor.

Finally, I went into the living room and stood in the doorway looking at her. She sat on the couch with tears in her eyes.

"Go ahead and cry about it. I think I am being fair. You fight, I fight. You're nice, I'm nice."

"I don't want to fight," she sobbed. "I want to have a normal life!"

"Ok, see? That's your choice. If you want normal, you've got normal."

"It doesn't work that way, John." The anger had crept back into her voice.

"It does with me."

"Fine. Fine! We'll do it your way. We always do anyway."

"Hey, do it your way. You want problems? Do it your way. It's your choice."

"Fine."

"You wanna take a walk?"

"No. I am tired. I want to sleep."

"That's fine," I said. So I took Charles out for a walk, and she went to bed for the rest of the day.

The rest of the weekend, things seemed to look up. She was tired, but we were living in the same house, so that seemed to be a lateral step to me. On Monday, I went to work and called mid-day. Everything was going fine. Maybe things would improve. I had put my foot down, and now we had an established boundary. I felt that this was a kind, rational, sane move. I was quite happy with myself.

That night I got home around dinner time. Cindi and Charles were nowhere to be found. "Hmmm..." I thought to myself. "Where are they?"

"Hello?" I called. "Cindi?"

Nothing. "Great," I said under my breath.

I went up the stairs. Perhaps it was a late naptime today.

On the floor of our room Cindi lay sprawled out, her face wet with tears. Charles was in his crib. In her hand was a paring knife. I quickly looked around the room and sized things up.

"Hey, what's up," I said calmly.

No response. Her eyes were closed, but there was no blood.

"Cindi, what's up?" I said more forcefully, but still calmly...I hoped.

Charles moved in his crib. He was alive.

She opened her eyes. Tears spilled out. "I don't want to be alive anymore," she said quietly. "I waited till you came home."

I got down on the floor as if to say something quietly but reached out and caught hold of the knife. "Let go," I said. She let go.

"I don't want to live. It's too hard," she said almost without air behind the words.

"What did you take?"

"Nothing."

"Advil? Aspirin? What did you eat?"

"Nothing."

"You sure?"

"I'm sure."

"Cause if you keel over in a minute from something you ate, I'm going to be pissed."

"I'm not going to keel over."

"You better not."

"I won't."

"Ok, get up. Sit up." She sat up on the bedroom floor. "Listen, I need you. Charles needs you. You are important. You decide your own destiny, but please don't shit on us."

"I can't do it anymore."

"Ok, get in bed. I am going to check on you every five minutes. Then we'll decide what to do together, ok? You can do that; I know you can."

"Fine."

I sat in the next room thinking, "This is who is watching my son? This is who I am counting on? What am I thinking?" I just sat there for about an hour trying to figure out what to do. It couldn't go on this way. This was crazy. Cindi was crazy! I was trusting a crazy person to make sane decisions for my child.

Cindi slept while I took care of Charles for the rest of the evening.

It was 10:00 PM, and Cindi was asleep. Charles was asleep. I had already pushed my new truck down the block and around the corner. My blood was one synchronized pulse going through my body as I walked into Charlie's dark room and carefully, quietly gathered him and his blankets into my arms. I quietly tiptoed down the stairs and out into the August night.

From the Abyss   John Emil Augustine

Escape

It was 11 pm and dark outside the city. Charles slept in his car seat in the truck as we roared up highway 5, west of the Twin Cities. Lights became sparser. Headlights now outnumbered streetlights.

My muffler had come apart shortly after I bought the truck, rust splitting the tailpipe about midway up. I had rolled and clamped sheet metal around the fault area, but the sound of the engine still escaped nonetheless. The little blue Chevy S-10 was really the one thing I owned now, I thought as I sat at a stoplight. Except for my clothes, I really had nothing. Everything had been absorbed, assimilated, or thrown away when I got married. It was strange to think this assembled conglomeration of plastic and rusted metal was the one thing I could use that was completely mine. The one thing Cindi would not actually want.

My folks heard me coming down the driveway, and I saw a light go on inside. Then the floodlight in the driveway came on. I pulled to a stop and slid the seat up to get at the car seat in back. My mom was outside in her bathrobe, watching me to see what was going on.

"Can we stay here for the night?"

"Yes. What's going on?"

I told her about the knife, the police, everything. We talked in the kitchen while I mixed a bottle for Charles. My mom suggested I go to the local police in the morning and report what had happened. She said if there were a suicide threat, they would have to investigate. They had a team for this kind of thing in every police department of every city. My mom worked in the courts. She was used to this kind of thing, only not in her own family.

The next morning, I called in sick, went to the local government building, and talked to the police chief. I reported what was going on; he called someone in the St. Paul police department. Within an hour they would be at my house. I was told to go back to my folks', and they would call me with information after the initial investigation occurred.

That afternoon, he called my folks' house and let me know St. Paul had sent their psyche team to my house to question Cindi. She was fine. I asked for clarification, and he said they had determined she was not going to kill herself. I wondered how they were able to predict the future so accurately and quickly. He said it was safe to bring the baby home as far as he knew.

The phone rang. It was for me. It was Cindi. She sounded…happy?

"I'm fine," she said. I could almost hear her smiling. This was so weird. Was she fine?

"Ok," I said. I had no idea what to do.

"You can come home."

"Ok."

Silence.

"You have to come home."

"Ok." My thoughts raced. Should I? Did I have to?

"I said bring Charles home." There was the anger I knew.

"I'm not sure. How do I know I'm not going to come home, and something will have happened?"

"Nothing will happen."

"How do I know that? You were there yesterday. You heard yourself. What am I supposed to think?"

"You are supposed to think that I need some help. Not fucking run away with my baby!"

"See, that's what I'm talking about. How do I know you're not going to get so pissed you do something to Charles?"

"I would never do that, and you know it!"

"I don't know it. What would you think if you were in my shoes?"

"I would be *trying to help!*"

"Ok. Fine. What can I do to help?"

"Come home. *Now!*"

"Jesus. Relax."

"You *have my child!* Relax? You are so sick, John. Get the fuck home with my child!"

"I am coming home."

"Good! You'd better. And you'd better not pull this shit again."

"What would you have done?"

"Get the fuck home with my child!"

"I told you I am coming home."

"*You better fucking come home!*"

The line went dead.

This was not the situation I wanted to bring my kid back into. What could I do?

I told my folks the cops had said Cindi was fine, and I had to go home with Charles. I'm not sure what they thought, but there wasn't much I could do. At least, I didn't think so. If I kept him away, that would then have been kidnapping since the police had given me the all clear to bring him back. But bringing Charles home to her was an extremely unsettling idea.

I got into my truck with Charles and fired it up. In the warming afternoon, I drove zombie-like back up the highway, trying to come up with some sort of plan, some way to protect Charles despite being out-maneuvered. I didn't have a chance in hell with the cops. They side with the mom. It would take a murder for anyone to pay attention, and then, were it Charles, it wouldn't matter. I could go quietly and never see her again. My truck, the only thing I really owned, would take me out of there.

I stopped the thought process and realized what I was thinking. If my wife were to murder my son? Had it really come to that? What was I supposed to do? I couldn't beat her; couldn't out-maneuver her because the cops were on her side. Despite what I had said, I was not happy with the prospect of going to jail. Again I stopped. Was I really there? I was worried about my wife sending me to jail? Into what kind of hell was this child going to grow up?

I had to play nice. She had out-maneuvered me. I couldn't match her. She could say one thing to me and another to the outside world, and I would not be believed. She could turn things so easily against me and then, *bam*, no dad for Charles.

I felt a bit like I was in a monster movie. I could hear a 1950s news anchor announcing, "Bullets can't stop it. Rockets can't stop it. We may need to use nuclear force." The movie was called *It Came from the Abyss,* and I was standing there with a revolver shooting ineffective bullets at "The Creature" with cardboard arms and one horrible eye.

Ineffective as my can-do attitude was, I knew I had to be a dad first and foremost. And being a dad meant, I guessed, being a patsy. I had to surrender for Charles. I had to toss all the weapons in my arsenal to the ground, because its horrible eye just kept going 'round. My one shot was to walk further into the relationship, unarmed. Once inside, maybe I could come up with something. I knew I was tying my own hands, but my surrender wouldn't work without the chains.

As I drove, I also began wondering if the suicide was bullshit or real. Cindi was tricky. Should I dismiss it altogether, or did I really need to watch for another suicide attempt? I couldn't risk that. And what about Charles? What would she do to him? Forget the suicide, what about Charles? I had to regain her confidence so I could keep tabs on her. Keep your friends close and your enemies closer. I finally understood that saying.

I stopped again. Was this really what it had come to? Cindi was my enemy, and I had to try to maneuver as in a chess game so that she would have no choice but to make certain moves? We were playing an advanced game of chess as adversaries? *This was marriage?* This was not a marriage. That was not what I had wanted. We were supposed to be a team!

"Son, I married her for better or for worse. For better or for worse." The words of my great-grandfather flashed through my head.

Downtown Minneapolis came into view: The Foshay Tower, the I.D.S. Center, the Metrodome.

We had to be a team. That was my angle! I had to convince her I was going to be on her team. I wanted to help her. That is what she was asking for. That's what a suicide attempt is. There's suicide, and there's the attempt. The attempt is a cry for help, of course! But how could I be there for her when I had to work?

I crossed the Mississippi River into Saint Paul.

I felt guilty for working all of a sudden. Yet, having called in sick that day, I also felt guilty for not working. I was damned either way. I was about to go down and had to take a breath and dive back into the abyss. There was no other way. But how? How could I work and not work simultaneously? How could I be at home and be at work? I couldn't phone in my lectures. Couldn't meet at the house. God, how I couldn't meet at the house. No one should be there, I thought. But if I could phone from work to the house, say, every hour. Wait, how could I do that? Every hour? That was crazy. If only Cindi could be convinced to phone me whenever she needed her teammate's help...but I would be in the middle of class. I had to think of a way. I just had to.

I was approaching the Snelling Avenue exit as I was thinking. Wait! I had an idea! WOW. The store just off 94 and Snelling, World of Wireless! A pager! This could be Cindi's instant connection to me regardless of what was going on. She could page me; I could take a break, solve the problem or create a stop-gap, then get back to work. If she would use it, it would hopefully bail Charles out if something were happening that Cindi could not handle. It had to work. It was my only idea, and I was almost home.

I pulled into the back lot of WOW, went in with Charles, and bought a pager and whatever kind of plan they had for pagers back in 2001. I had to frame the idea the right way for Cindi. This just might work.

From the Abyss   John Emil Augustine

Recapture

It was a bit like a cow walking into the slaughter house, except the cow, in my case, had a chance to talk himself out of it. That's how it felt, anyway. No one is going to spare the cow, but still...a talking cow. How could she not listen to a talking cow?

Walking into my house had become an emotional chore. I would go through a familiar series of events: fast heartbeat, sweating, ears ringing, short breaths, dizziness, sudden and extreme fear of the unknown. This was becoming normal for me as I drove the last few blocks to my house, and it would happen almost every day.

Cindi snatched Charles away from me and went through an "Are you ok?" routine with him. He was fine, but the scene needed to be played.

"I want a divorce," she snapped.

"Right out of the gate," I thought to myself. No time to explain the pager or anything.

"I want a divorce, and I want it tomorrow. You get the paperwork together, and I will sign it. Do you understand?"

"We're not getting a divorce."

"You will *get the paperwork,* and I will *sign!*" she screamed.

Charles began to cry. This was not going well.

"Look, we're not getting a divorce. We have to clean the slate, so we can work together. We have to be a team: you, me, and Charles. We are a team, and we can do this."

"Oh," she laughed. "We are *not* a team, John."

"I know we're not a team, but I have to be sure we get back to being a team. We've come too far to give up. We have to work together, not against each other."

"We can work together on getting a divorce. I've had it."

"We are not getting a divorce."

"If you won't get the paperwork together, then I *will!*"

"I won't sign it, so forget it."

"The court will *make you sign, John!*"

"Jesus, why do you want a divorce so bad?"

"You kidnapped my child!"

"It's not kidnapping if he comes back the next day."

"We'll let the judge decide that."

"Jesus Christ, Cindi. That's why you want a divorce?"

"I have wanted a divorce from day one, and you know it, John. *From day one!*"

"Day one? Which day was that? Before the wedding?"

"Yes, and you know it was."

"Well that's dumb. You wanted a divorce before we got married?"

"You knew I did."

"Before we got married?"

"*You knew I did!*"

"Good Lord! So this is about money? You could have gotten me to pay child support without the marriage."

"I know that!"

"So what…spousal support? Really?"

"I don't care about support! I just want you out!"

"Well, we have to work through this. You want me out now, but I'm not leaving. When you calm down, we will figure this out."

"When I calm down? You're accusing me of trying to take your…what…vast sums of money you make at your shitty teaching job at a fake college? Then you tell me to calm down?"

"I'm not telling you to calm down. We will talk about this later."

I went into the kitchen, ran dishwater into the sink, and threw in the sponge. I heard keys and quickly the front door slammed. I grabbed a plate and dunked it into the water.

Now what?

Familiar Voice

Thus began the cold war. I wasn't leaving, and she had come back and wasn't leaving either. I moved to the couch, she to the rest of the house. I was not going to leave Charles unattended for long. Every chance she got, she dug into me. If I got mad, I was the bad guy. If I ignored her, I was the bad guy. If I tried to appease her, she was indifferent. That was the best response, indifference. I grew to love indifference.

Still, I was able to teach, to keep my job. Cindi did like the idea of the pager after she calmed down. Unfortunately, she mostly liked it because she could get me at any time and tell me off. I would cancel class because she would page with the message "911" which was the code for an emergency. It would begin as an emergency, but there was always something I had done or not done or should do or should not do or had not done or should not have done. I couldn't win. But in not winning, I was shifting her focus from suicide to being pissed off at me, and I was still able to spend time with my son.

I did agree that we were officially separated. Cindi actually made me say it. I didn't see the point, but she insisted I say it.

So I said, "Fine, we're separated. But I'm not leaving."

The living room was my new home, and the couch was my new bed. She began talks with a free lawyer through Legal Aid, and I came home every day to be sure she didn't hurt Charles or kill herself.

The couch was a multi-sectional. I remember lying across three sections while they drifted apart throughout the night. Evenings were hard. Once Charles was asleep, Cindi would go up to her room, and I would watch TV in the living room until I was tired. It was hard to be tired because I was always on edge. Often, Cindi would come down and pester me, telling me she was filing for divorce or telling me the cops were on their way. Sleep was not easy. I was tired, always. I began dragging through life.

Not only was I tired, but I was becoming beaten down. When you hear how much someone hates you and how much of a deadbeat you are because you sleep on a couch; that wears on you after a while. At work, I would stop class, answer the page, hear about whatever problem Cindi had with me at the moment, hang up the phone, walk back to the classroom, and try to make walking through the doorway the difference between sad and happy. I would try to turn it on like a light switch.

The minute I got into the classroom, I would become that other person, the one the students liked and were curious about. What was I like outside the classroom? Had I ever smoked pot? Was I from New York? Did I ever do standup? Did I make up all my own exercises? I never liked that kind of attention. It never mattered because I had that threat clipped to my belt, that invisible chain which dragged me farther and farther down. Every time the pager went off, the tug was sharper and harder, the reemerging from the murky negativity less likely – the fight back through the classroom doorway, from sad to happy, a constant and tiring Houdini-like struggle.

What problems Cindi brought up! I spent too much on coffee, so I bought a coffee maker and a thermos. Charles' head was misshapen, so I helped Cindi find a cranial sacral therapist. Something needed repair, and I hadn't gotten to it. So I got to it. The guys were calling asking if I could play a gig, and Cindi didn't want me to, so I would call and turn it down. Everything that came up, I said, "This is my fault, and I have to make it right." That is what a people pleaser does. I would look at what I was doing and change it to suit her. We were separated, but she and Charles were still my life. So I played the role of a goalie trying to catch every puck. But everyone knows a goalie can't catch every shot that comes in. And the minute I missed one, I would end up in big trouble.

Maybe I would still forget to repair the shingles. Maybe I would buy a coffee at the school anyway. Maybe I would agree to play a gig that was really important to the guys. There were many missteps. I was far less than a perfect husband to Cindi even though we were separated. I would find out that no amount of separation would matter. I would always be on the hook. I would always be condemned.

Then September 11th happened. A student who was two hours late for class came in at the last minute to jot down the day's homework and said a plane had hit a building in New York. Later, when everyone found out the extent of what was happening that day, I called Cindi, and we made a plan to meet up if we should need to evacuate the Twin Cities. It was the only constructive conversation we had that autumn. After that, Cindi bought both of us cell phones. Thinking back, I bet they would look pretty funny now with their retractable antennas, big buttons, and tiny screens. As limited as those phones were by today's standards, they did make the pager obsolete to me as a result. The world was changing despite my being mired in my own problems.

Two weeks later, I was served with papers at our house. Cindi had officially filed for divorce. I had to show up in court. I had to get a lawyer. I had to spend a ton of time and money. But I didn't have to leave, so I didn't. I stayed on the couch, trying to protect Charles. Every day became worse. I just had to take it. I kept thinking I could take it. Whenever I left the house, an overwhelming moment of happiness would quickly turn into despair because I knew my escape would be short-lived. I kept the few clothes I had in my truck. Every day when I got home to find my key still opened the front door, I was surprised. The evenings that Cindi said little or nothing to me were like a breath of fresh lilacs in the dead of winter. Coming home and finding the house intact always seemed like a miracle.

I was becoming very thin. I just didn't have time or energy. Nothing tasted very good, so I just didn't eat much. My belt had eight sets of punched holes that I had made each time I had to fight with my pants to keep them up. Anyway, there wasn't much money for my food. The lawyer who had been recommended to me by my mom's friend in the courts asked for a $3000 retainer. I lived on Mountain Dew and energy bars.

One morning in late September, between classes, my phone rang. I had no idea who would call me on that phone, but when I looked, it said, "Maggie." I had programmed everyone's phone number I knew into it so I could throw away my cheap rolodex which had coffee stains and never closed anymore.

"Hello?"

"John?"

"Yeah. Who is this?"

"It's Maggie."

"Oh yeah. My phone said Maggie, but I wasn't sure."

"Do you have a minute or two to talk?"

"What is Maggie calling me for?" I thought. I hadn't talked to her in years. "Sure. I'm actually on break."

"This is a little weird, but I decided I had better call and talk to you. I decided it was the right thing to do."

"Ok. Sure. Whatever it is, it's ok, Maggie."

"I know. I know you will understand this."

"Sure."

I had been walking down the hall to my office and now shut the door and sat down in my chair. I looked out onto the deck where a few students, faculty, and kitchen crew were smoking. Puffs of smoke rose into the cooling September air.

"This morning I was sleeping, and my phone rang. You accidentally called me."

"Oh, gee, I'm sorry about that. I just got this phone and don't really know how to use it."

"That's ok. I could tell it was in your pocket. Must have just dialed by mistake."

"Guess so. Sorry about that."

"Well, here's the weird part. I was going to hang up, but I recognized your voice, so I tried to get your attention."

"Oh! I didn't hear you."

"I know. And I'm sorry, but I just listened for a minute. Then I heard a woman. Was that your girlfriend?"

"Well, it was probably Cindi, my wife."

"John, I'm sorry I listened in on your conversation, but I did."

"Oh, that's ok."

"Does she always talk to you like that?"

"Huh?"

"She was horrible to you. Is that how she is?"

"I guess so, yeah," I had to admit it. Even after a few years, I couldn't hide anything from Maggie. And it wouldn't have mattered anyway. She already knew.

"John, I am saying this as your friend."

"Ok."

"This does not sound like a healthy relationship."

"No, I guess it's not."

"I hope you don't mind my doing this, but I felt that if you were in trouble and didn't know it, I had to say something."

"I appreciate it."

"Do you know this? Do you understand that this isn't healthy for you?"

"Yeah, I know."

"John, you have to do something."

"Ok."

"You sound terrible. Are you ok?"

"I'm ok."

"Tell me you're not living with her."

"I am."

"John, you have to stop. I'm sorry, but if what I heard is normal, you have to get out."

"I know."

"Well, I said my piece and want you to know I love you. I know you'll do the right thing."

"Ok, I love you too, Maggie. Thanks."

"Thanks for listening."

It was like having a doctor tell you that if you don't quit smoking you will die in a year. Nonetheless, you're stuck smoking and can't figure out a way to quit. It was as hopeless as it gets. Still, it was nice to hear a friendly voice. I replayed the conversation over and over at night on the sectional, just to remember Maggie's balanced, level-headed, sweet voice as many times as I could.

From the Abyss   John Emil Augustine

Total Eclipse

> Date: Tue Oct 16, 2001, 10:47 am
> Subject: Barn Party
> Hello, fans:
>
> This Saturday the 20th our band will be on stage at Scott Youngstead's farm. As you know, appearances by our group are rare these days, and this will likely be the last one until our CD release party which will be in a few months. We will use the proceeds from the Barn Party to fund what is left of our CD production process (pressing the CDs and printing the covers). $10 gets you all the food, beer, and music you can handle. Pig roast, 15 kegs, and plenty of good ol' fashion homemade food! Scott is donating all the proceeds to the production of our CD!!! Tell your friends because we want to make this a kick-ass party! More information including directions will come later this week.
>
> Hope to see you there!

This was the email I sent out from work, in the midst of the craziness I was experiencing, for our third-to-last show. Actually, some of my students knew Scott and were planning to go to see "Augustine" rock the barn. I was a little uneasy whenever there were students at my gigs. I never really knew how it got out, but it was almost inevitable. There was a website. I suppose once they knew the name of my band, they could find out whatever they wanted on the Internet. I figured I could not stop them, so I tried to ignore the situation and not act like a bad role model at the gigs.

Still, on my way to the farm about an hour northwest of the Twin Cities, I stopped and got a big bottle of Meyers's Rum and a two-liter of Coke. I wasn't planning to get hammered, but I needed a night that would be like the old days. And I needed numbness. I needed to shut off my phone and party with the guys. We wouldn't be able to do it much longer. We had our CD release show coming and then, just maybe, one last farewell show.

The Youngsteads had a pig roasting on a huge outdoor rotisserie. I remember the smell. This was a good, old-fashioned barn party with great food donated by moms and grandmas, kegs on ice, kids running around – such a nice change of pace. It was a warm October afternoon: mid-60s and sunny. The smell in the air, a mixture of leaves and hay, of campfire smoke and cooking pork, of earth and crisp, changing air. Leaves were beginning to lose their green, eclipsed by yellows and oranges. Brown and red tipped leaves hung overhead and blew wistfully across the soft grass. Around the farmhouse and the barn were things you might hope to see on a mid-October afternoon: pumpkins and gourds on stoops and hay bales, small decorative scarecrows hanging here and there, black and orange party streamers strung about the barn where the tables sat. These things meant we were all welcome and that the family was happy to be hosting the party. It was all such a refreshingly good scene to take in.

I loved warm October afternoons. I had on a long sleeve shirt and black bell-bottomed pants, black boots, and what had come to be my show hat: a colorful African Kufi. In my truck back: ice, Meyers's Rum, Coke, and plastic cups. At least this one last time, I would exist within a small slice of reprieve, a moment of simple goodness and fun.

It was getting dark, and the rest of the band began to pour beers and get waters for onstage (usually two beers and a bottle of water got us through the first set). We had a last smoke then began to pick up instruments and jam a bit, in essence quietly calling people over. There wasn't actually a stage that night, just a long tarp next to the barn. We played under it just in case it rained. It didn't, but our instruments and gear were safe anyway. Scott and his family had thought of everything.

I just remember lots of people coming over: old and young people sitting, standing, drinking and smoking; dancing and talking once in a while to the person next to them as they watched and listened. It was a nice feeling. It was as if, for a moment, I had never messed up, had never ruined my life, and had never met Cindi.

In truth, I never even thought the word, "Cindi" while playing. It was nice to forget. After we played for an hour and a half, it was about 10:00, and we took a break, promising to return in half an hour after we re-beered. Everyone spread out and got more food and beer, wandered, smoked, chatted, and went to their cars to smoke herb. I went over to the campfire and ran into some of my students. We chatted and joked, jabbed back and forth. I gave them the "Don't tell our administration that I have a band" shtick. It was fun, and I had a good buzz going. As I was standing there joking, I noticed a face I had never seen before. That in itself was not unusual, but what was a little unusual was the face kept glancing at me.

I have to tell you, at this point in life I wanted nothing to do with girls because of my situation with the divorce, and because I had been there and done that enough times to steer clear of girls who decided our band was "The Best." Girls were not hard to find, and I shirked them; hated them in a way. Every girl would turn out to be a Cindi or an Elizabeth or a Maggie or whoever had flaked or turned to shit on me. So a girl glancing at me made me very uncomfortable. Some chicks could be hard to ward off.

The only thing was, when she turned and talked to someone standing next to her, I took a good look anyway. The blonde hair made me do it, I guess. Her face looked soft. Her hair looked soft. Her eyes were friendly and sweet. Her smile was gorgeous and her lips….

Shit! Just then she looked over and caught me gawking. I hoped my mouth wasn't open with drool running out the side! I quickly smiled, put my head down, and moved elsewhere around the fire. She wasn't for me, really. Just some chick. I walked out of her line of vision and took up a conversation with one of my students: an older guy who had nerve damage in his legs from a car accident. His pals called him Chronic long after he had given up booze and weed. He was about 40 and had a good outlook on life, he said, because of his drunk-driving accident. He couldn't feel his legs, but had taught himself to walk again anyway; then he promptly enrolled in college. He wasn't letting that little problem stop him. He was letting it inspire him, actually. We often talked after class. He was completely genuine, and I liked him.

We talked about the night, cooling now but still comfortable. Beautiful weather, really, we agreed. The blonde chick had worked her way around the fire, across from me again, and was glancing at me and Chronic.

"Hey," he said quietly. "She's looking at you."

"Who?"

"Dude, open your eyes. Look at the blonde across from us. She digs you, man."

"Yeah, great."

"Go over there, dude."

"Come on, Chronic. I'm in the middle of a divorce. You think I want to add another chick to the mix? Come on."

"Dude, your wife is a bitch, right?"

"Yeah, she's a bitch, all right." I looked at my boots. This conversation suddenly sucked.

"Well, get on with the divorce, and in the meantime, go hit on that chick. I shouldn't say chick; she is cool. That's my buddy's girlfriend's friend. She is awesome, man. I said I was thirsty, and she went and got me a beer a while ago. I didn't even ask. She just went and did it. She's really nice. You *gotta* go over there."

"Yeah, I don't know."

"I *do* know, man. You're stupid if you don't go over there."

"Ok, I'll think about it."

"Look, she's looking over here again. That's three times. Dude, she wants you. You're stupid."

"Dude, I'll think about it."

"Don't think about it. That's just you being a stupid chicken."

"Ok. Jesus, Chronic, it's a wonder you let me get a word in edgewise during class."

"Hey, that's because I respect you, man. That's why I'm telling you this now. You, of all the people I know, should get some happiness."

"Ok. I'm going to get another beer."

"Great. I'll come with and introduce you."

"Naw, don't worry about it. I got it."

I went over to the keg...well, stack of kegs... and poured a beer. As I turned, I saw Chronic talking to the blonde and pointing at me. "That bastard," I thought. I turned and walked away, over to the stage. I fiddled with my Rhodes. I'd had a problem with one of the keys during the first set, so I was trying to see if it was stuck or broken.

Chronic stiffly walked over on the legs he could not feel. "Hey, dumbass, what the hell are you doing? I was just talking to that girl. Her name is Kim. Dude, she wants to talk to you."

"Chronic, stop. Enough!" I yelled, angry.

"OK, sorry, man. I'm just trying to help. Seriously, she is so nice. I'm just trying to help." He shook his head and walked away.

As I finished putting my Rhodes back together, I started to feel bad. I got pushed around enough as it was at home, but this was just Chronic trying to be nice. I went back to where he sat by the fire.

"Sorry, Chronic."

"No, it's cool, man. No hard feelings."

There she was looking at me again. Chronic had said her name, but I couldn't remember it.

She walked away from the crowd and stood against a fence by the woods. I barely glanced, and she smiled again. "Crap," I thought. God, but she was cute. What kept going through my head was the fact that she had gotten Chronic a beer. No personal gain intended, she was just nice. "Man," I wondered. "How can I get some of that?"

"But I could," I thought. "She wanted to talk to me. Maybe I could." We looked at each other again. This time we both smiled, and I put my head down shyly. "But I couldn't," I thought. "Someone nice cannot be allowed to meet me. I am a walking death trap. No new people should know me. Enough people are affected by my problems as it is."

But she was so sweet looking. Her glance met mine again. "I had better do something," I thought. "It's now or never."

Just then one of the guys from around the fire walked up to her and started talking. "Ah, problem solved," I thought. "If she's looking to meet someone, there we go. Whew! That was close.

Jesus, I almost went over there." I drank the rest of my beer from the plastic cup.

Someone said something to me, and I half-engaged in a conversation. With one eye, I glanced over at the blonde girl and the guy she had just met. Things were going well for those two; it looked like they were hitting it off. That was kind of nice, I thought. Steering her my way was not one of Chronic's best ideas, well-intended as it was. I continued joking with a couple guys as I stood there with my empty cup. This was a good night, and I had just avoided a crisis.

But it struck me how I longed for the kindness described by Chronic, the kindness embodied in her or a similar girl. I couldn't be allowed such kindness. It would be like someone outstretching her hand to a shark attack victim and being pulled down herself. "Forget reaching out your hand," I thought. "I'm not pulling anyone else down with me."

Then something unexpected happened. As I was standing there by the fire, singing part of "Brick in the Wall," with a couple of the guys, I noticed the blonde girl trying to get rid of the guy who had walked up to her. "Gee, poor guy," I thought. It wasn't long before he split. "Man, he was shut down! This chick is particular. Wonder if anyone else will try," I mused.

"Crap. I was thinking about her. This is not good. She looked at me again. Damn it." The internal struggle was tough. She liked me; that was obvious. I was intrigued; I had to admit that. But so often people think they like each other, and then they meet…

And then they meet!

I knew how to repel her! I know that sounds kind of sad and mean, but I had done it with Maggie, and I could do it with this girl. I only had to meet her, and who the hell cared what I said? This was perfect. I would be awful. She looked again. I stayed and forced myself, smiling, to look for more than a second. She smiled. We both looked down and then up again. Then she did something I couldn't resist. She made the tiniest motion with her head. "Come over here a sec," it said.

The minute I introduced myself, all bets were off. Her voice, the sweetest voice I had ever heard, completely blew my plan. That voice eclipsed everything I had previously known or thought about her. Her voice: softly adorable, sincere, slightly excited, truly happy, fun, new, yet familiar. There was suddenly nothing else in the world. No autumn, no leaves, no students, no party, no Cindi, no worries, nothing. I knew the voice was the most exciting and comfortable thing I could ever wish for. I just stood there and fell into it, like falling into an event you happen upon; you look up and the moon begins to disappear. The shadow of the earth washes over it; it is gone and you can't believe it, yet you do because you are there, immersed in it. I wanted her voice. I wanted to keep it. How could I harness the voice of this beautiful and sweet girl? How could I revisit it, replay it, over and over and over?

Just then, the guys started our traditional 'heading toward the stage' routine. "C'mon" calls began and handfuls of beers were carefully carried toward the stage. I had ten minutes.

Suddenly what I said *did* matter.

From the Abyss   John Emil Augustine

One Ticket to Paradise

Not much of a slick talker, I just said what I was thinking. "Hey, do you like Meyers's Rum?"
"What?"
"Rum and Coke. Do you like Rum and Coke?"
"I don't know."
"Well the band is about to start playing again, but I am going to my truck to make a Rum and Coke before our set. Want to walk with me? I'll share some."
"Sure."
"Well," I thought, "that was her out and she didn't take it. This will either move quickly or fall flat. Either way, I gotta get a Rum and Coke and get onstage."
So we walked through the darkened, sparse woods into the Youngsteads' backyard where everyone had parked. My truck was in the middle of the cars with my drinking supplies in the back.
"Ok, this is Myers's Rum. Smell." I took the cap off the bottle and held it up to her nose.
"Ew. I don't think I like rum."
"Ok. You can have a sip of mine before you decide."
"You have all this stuff in the back of your truck? That's funny."
I poured the Rum and Coke into a plastic cup. "Yeah, I guess it is kinda funny. I needed a little more than beer to keep me going tonight. Try." I held the cup out to her.
"Ok." She took a sip. "Woo! That's strong."
"You like it?"
"I don't know yet."
"Well, you don't have to like it, but hold that cup for a bit until you decide. You don't have to know right now."
She took another drink. "I kinda like it, actually."
"If you don't, that's ok. It's all I drink other than beer." I had begun to fill an extra-large Mountain Dew bottle with my concoction.
"Yeah, I like it. It's kind of sweet and also seems strong; sort of mysteriously delicious."

"Yeah? I guess that about sums it up."

She stood with her back against my driver's side door, sipping as I finished mixing my bottle of booze.

"This is nice."

"What? The drink?"

"No, this…you."

The band was going on very soon. It was now or never. "Do you want to kiss me?"

"What? No!"

"I think you do."

"Now?"

"If not now, when?"

"No!"

"Why else did you come over here?" I took a step closer, and she stayed where she was.

"I don't know."

"Well, just try it. You don't have to decide anything, just give it a try."

"I'm just not sure." We were moving closer to one another. Intentionally or unintentionally, we were drifting together, very slowly.

"Try."

"Ok."

Her lips were soft; sweet with rum. My hand reached for her cheek and my fingers found her hair. She showed no sign of pulling away. Carefully, almost in protest with herself, she put her arms around my back, plastic cup in hand. We held on for a moment, then she pulled away, and I backed up a half step.

"Did you like it?"

"I don't know yet."

This was good. We were playing music with an echo. It was natural. We were neither trying nor not trying. We just were. Together; existing in the moment in harmony and in unison. This was art. This was collaborative improvisation. We had a theme with emerging variations. These were the chances I took on stage knowing the band would catch me. I was beginning to see this was someone who might take chances with me and catch me as well.

"It's ok if you don't know yet. C'mon, hold on again, and have another try."

"Ok."

We embraced again, readily this time. It was a paradise into which I had fallen and no longer cared from where. Only that it was; only that this existed.

Then she broke away again, more slowly. "You ok?" I asked.

"Yeah."

"Do you like it?"

"Actually, yes, I kinda do." She smiled. Her smile was a supermodel's smile, the kind that could light up a magazine cover. It washed over me, and I stood in it, delighted and admiring.

The band started. "Shit. I gotta get over there."

"Give me one more."

"Rum and Coke?"

"No, silly. This…" Her hand found the back of my head, and she moved toward my lips again for another sweet, intoxicating taste.

"Kim!" A girl's voice came from a nearby car. She pulled away and looked behind her.

"Just a sec!" she called.

"What are you doing?" the voice called.

"Just a sec!"

"You have to go, huh?" I asked.

"Yeah. So do you."

"Yeah." Suddenly, I realized where I was and how close I was to being pulled from this paradise back to the fiery putrid hell in which I actually existed. I had fallen into paradise, but now the cable to which I was attached was about to snap tight and pull me painfully back, fight as I may.

"Kim! Quit making out, and get over here! We have to go!" the female voice called again.

"Coming!" she yelled to the darkness behind us, not moving from her position between my truck and me. "I have to go."

By now the band was jamming, and we both were being pulled in opposite directions. She finally stepped away and grabbed for her purse in the back of the truck.

"Kim," I said, as if I were waking from a dream which I could still see and feel as I drifted away from it.

"What?"

"We're both being pulled away. How can I talk to you again?"

"Here." She put her purse on the hood of my truck, reached for a pen and a torn receipt, and carefully wrote her email address on it. "Email me."

"I will."

"Good!" she half-yelled as she ran to her friend's car. I topped off my Mountain Dew bottle with rum while listening to the band jam. Then I watched her friend's car pull away, the girls inside animatedly talking to her, asking what she had been doing, I supposed. Then I hurried over to join the band with the email address tucked carefully into my wallet. It was my one ticket back to paradise.

Coming Clean

I arrived at the perpetual black hole which was my house and let the usual agony at being back re-engulf me. But along with the agony was a twinge of hope that turned quickly to regret. I couldn't drag this poor girl into all this. She was so sweet and warm, so nice. She was the perfect person to not know me. The perfect person to never have met me.

But she had. Damn it. She had met me, and now she liked me. I had to stop this before it started. I had to be a good person and let her off the hook quickly. Forget paradise; that place didn't exist for me. Never could. Not with the sewage that I was mired in, not with this mess I had created for myself. Wanting something was one thing. The reality of pursuing it was quite another.

I lay there on the sectional couch, losing my buzz and trying to figure out what to do about Kim. I had her email address. She didn't have mine. I could just not send an email, and the situation would go away. Yes, the easy and painless way! But she was so sweet. I just couldn't do that. I had to explain somehow. She deserved it.

I had to explain. That was it: I would tell the truth and explain my situation! She would understand. Or she wouldn't. Either way, it was my best choice, I figured. The truth would set me free…or in this case, release me back into my captivity. I would apologize for being a player, tell her what was going on, and then say, "Sorry…see ya."

The next day, I sat down at my desk at work and began my email:

> *Subject: Kim, Please Accept My Apology*
>
> *Kim,*
>
> *I am sorry about last night. I really did enjoy our time. I think you are awesome, and I do appreciate your attention. I don't get that kind of attention anymore. Well, this is a*

shitty way to start an email, but I feel I have to do the right thing.

Here's the problem: I am neck-deep in a horrible situation, and I just can't get involved, even a little, with anyone. I know that's an asshole thing to say, but I do hope you will read on so that you'll understand why I am writing this. If not, I will understand and don't really expect a reply.

Anyway, here goes: I have a son. He is six months old. His name is Charles. I have a wife. We are separated and are getting a divorce. You see how complicated this is already, but there's more, so I hope you read on and understand why I kissed you and why I am writing this now.

I am always afraid for my son's safety. My wife has threatened to kill herself and has left a few times, so even though we are in the middle of a divorce, I am still staying at the house because I have to come home each day and make sure Charles is ok. I sleep on the couch in the living room. It is awful, to say the least.

I worry that I'll come home and find my wife and son gone or see that she has killed herself. I just don't know what will happen. I am trying to get Charles out of the house, but it is not easy. So you can see, at least a little, what a horrible hell I am in and why I have to write this and tell you I am sorry.

And I am sorry. I think you are incredible and was so truly happy during the short time we spent together. It really was wonderful, and I am sorry to be such a player with you. I really made a bad choice, and I wish I could reverse it. I had that one moment, our moment, when I was happy. And it is hell, I am finding out, to go back. But it is best that I do and that we don't write to or see each other again as I asked to do last night. Believe me when I say thank you for the moment. I only wish the circumstances were different. Again, I am sorry to be that asshole guy who does this. I just got caught up in the moment, and I hope you aren't too mad at me.

Love & Mercy,
John

"Whew!" I thought. "Hope that isn't too melodramatic, but it's the truth. I can at least say I was honest and up-front, player as I was."

Actually, writing that letter really cleared my conscience. I may have been a deadbeat, an asshole, a sick motherfucker, a bastard, a fucked up piece of shit, and everything else Cindi called me every day, but I was able to come clean and be honest with a girl I had mistakenly kissed because I had gotten caught up in the moment at a gig. I thought that was at least a half-point in my favor.

In the meantime, while this little saga with Kim began and ended, I was told I had to create a case against Cindi that was believable enough that a judge would look twice and at least consider letting Charles live with me. The negativity made me incredibly uncomfortable. Even if it was Cindi, I just hated to slam someone and take her kid. That just seemed so polarizing, almost unconscionably ruthless. It was a very tough thing to make myself do, but I had to think of Charles's safety.

So I headed to the landscaper, my old job, because I needed some negative character references about Cindi. I walked in, found Emily, and asked if she had a few minutes to talk.

"John!" She jumped up from her desk to hug me. "Yes, of course! How are you?"

"Well, not too good. I need to ask a favor."

"What is it?"

"Well, Cindi and I are getting a divorce."

"No!" She gasped, then covered her mouth and looked around the office. She grabbed my hand and whispered, "Come on, let's talk somewhere else." Then, a little louder, she said, "Take a walk with me, Duke. I missed you!" She pulled on my hand, smiling at the secretary as we passed, and soon we were walking toward the ball and burlap tree lot where there were fewer ears. The day was sunny and beautiful, like Emily. "What do you need me to do, John?"

"Well, I am worried about my son, Charles. Cindi has threatened to kill herself and leave us or leave with Charles, so I have to build a case against her in order to get Charles in my custody, so he'll be safe."

"Oh my goodness!" Emily's curly red hair glowed in the autumn sunlight.

"Yeah, it's not something I am looking forward to."

"Couldn't you get her some medication or some kind of help?"

"We tried that, and she quit the meds. Whenever I bring it up, she gets pissed at me. I just don't bring it up anymore. I can't really convince her of anything. She just wants me out."

"So...out of what?"

"I am still living in our house. I stay on the couch at night. I'm afraid if I don't go home every night, something will happen to Charles."

"Oh my God, John! This is terrible."

"Well, we will get through it. I guess we are getting a divorce, but I want to make it work out somehow. I don't want to take him. Not really. I just want the kid to be safe."

"Yes. I totally understand. Oh my God!" She seemed truly exasperated. "So what do you need from me?"

"I guess a letter, if it's possible, about her character. Weird or disturbing things you noticed while she worked here. I know how awful that sounds."

"Ok..." She thought for a minute.

"I'm sorry to even have to ask. I've never done this before and don't really want to, but this is what the lawyer is asking for."

"Lawyer...oh, Duke!" She hugged me. "This is so sad."

"It's ok, really. I just have to be careful what I do, so I don't mess things up for Charles."

"Ok, so you need a letter."

"Is there any way you could talk to Lisa or some of the other girls? Maybe they could write a letter too, or you could jog each other's memory a bit."

"Ok, yes, I will talk to Lisa and the girls. Oh, I am so sorry. I feel partially responsible. I hope you're doing ok."

"Yeah, I'm fine. It's a tough place to be, and I don't really know what to do, but I'll figure it out."

"Oh, John." She hugged me again.

"Thanks." It was so nice to have a hug. Not arousing, just a good feeling from someone I admired. But I realized at that moment how I had been mesmerized with Emily, not necessarily Cindi, when we were first going out. It was a ghastly thought, and quite perplexing. I loved Emily's straight-forwardness and her beautiful curly, red hair. I loved her up-beat, good-naturedness. She was magnetic. She was the reason for Cindi. I wished Cindi were her. I had the whole time.

"Alright, Duke, I have to get back. What is your phone number? I'll call you in a few days."

We went back to her office where I wrote down my number, then headed to class. When I got to my desk, I took a stack of papers out of my tote bag and got my desk situated with coffee and pen to do some fine-toothed combing through my next classes' rough drafts.

Then I sipped my coffee, ate a granola bar, and checked my inbox.

There was one new message: *Subject: Re: Kim, Please Accept My Apology.*

From the Abyss   John Emil Augustine

The Opposite Decision

> *John,*
> *Yes, I understand why you kissed me. I am glad you explained. You're not a player.*
> *This is not a good situation you are in. I want you to know I really liked meeting you, and we don't have to have a romantic relationship. But I am always here if you need me.*
> *Kim*

"I'll be damned," I thought. I guess I assumed she would be angry. But it dawned on me that I was more or less unimportant to her. She could probably take me or leave me. It was nice to be off the hook, and if I could have admitted it to myself at the time, slightly disappointing. Our moment, to her, was probably not much of anything. Still, our moment being so trivial to her was actually a good thing, I decided.

I guess it made sense that the moment was more important to me than to her. She probably had a million guys after her. Girls like her don't go after guys because they have a great pick as it is. They don't have to expend any effort. Any set of personality traits, physical traits, spiritual traits – she could pick from all the guys who came her way. That I knew. I guess it was liberating. I was mostly glad she was not mad. And it was kind of nice to have someone tell me I wasn't a complete jerk. I decided to tell her that.

> *Kim,*
> *I am just glad you're not pissed at me. I tend to forget there are people out there who are nice! Glad you wrote back and told me not to worry about it.*

> *You're right, the situation is not good, but I am stuck. The fewer people who know about it and have contact with me, the better. I already have had to drag people into this because I am trying to make a case against my wife so that I can get custody of Charles...just to keep him safe. I feel responsible for anyone who knows me and who knows about this. I guess I should not have told you anything, but I felt I had to explain. But no need to worry about me. As for you, there are a lot of cool guys out there, guys without all this awfulness going on. You have no kids, so get out there and enjoy yourself! Great to meet you.*
> *John*

It was then that I realized I couldn't drag people into this. I had already called my mom too many times in the middle of the night asking for advice. My dad had actually called me and told me to stop it because my calls kept her up and made her miserable. He was right. Nobody should have to go through this with me. I had made my bed. I had taken off the training wheels and now had to fall. No one could do that for me. No one should. Some things you have to go your own on. Some things are too horrible to share. I was already sharing this with Cindi. I was, as she said, selfish, always hoping someone would bail me out. And I had just pulled Emily into it. Jeez, what was wrong with me? I was stupid, just as I was told regularly. It was true: I really didn't think of anyone but myself. I cringed at the thought of what I had become.

Or had I been like this all along? Had I been selfish my whole life and was just now finally, truly realizing it? If so, that meant Cindi was right. She was probably right about a lot of things. She knew me. She knew how I was. This was how I was, a selfish and lazy person who was only into himself and his music and who never did the right thing. It was true, I realized. I could no longer hide from the truth.

When Emily called and asked me to lunch, I went. She said everyone would be willing to write a single letter encompassing the total experience of the department with Cindi. I told her I really appreciated her effort, but things were going better with Cindi, and we had decided to settle out of court and work together. It wasn't true, but I just wanted everyone to be let off the hook and feel good about it, or rather, forget about it. I remember watching Emily get into her car behind the restaurant. I really loved her. That was to be my last glimpse of her.

Then I was on my own again. No help from my folks, no help from Emily, no help from the Elizabeths, Maggies, and Kims of the world. You get help of some kind, and you begin to believe you need and/or deserve it. That was a slippery slope I had begun to fall into, and it was time to grab on, pull myself out of it, and stand up for myself, by myself. I believed in pulling myself up by my bootstraps, and now was the time. I knew I deserved what I was getting. I was who Cindi said I was, and I had to live with that fact. I had to work harder, do better, and help her in whatever way I could. I had to quit being selfish. In essence, I had to quit being me.

Cindi was asking for the most child support and spousal support that I could legally give. This was what I would agree to do. She was asking me to give her my half of the house. I would agree to do that, too. She was asking that I keep her and Charles on my healthcare, so I would. She was asking to claim Charles as her dependent every year on her taxes. What did I care? If she wanted it, it was the least I could do after being such an asshole for so long. It was depressing to realize all this, but at least I had.

When I got home that night, Cindi announced that she was planning to start a daycare in the house and needed to bring it up to whatever standards daycares had to adhere to. If I was to continue sleeping on her couch, I would need to pull my weight and make the place ready. It needed a lot of work. At least I had a chance to prove myself less of a deadbeat, I thought. I could do this. It was really the least I could do, I reasoned. After all, I was the problem. That was becoming more and more apparent.

I eventually paid for all the daycare supplies as well. Had I quit making payments on the house and moved out, Cindi would have been screwed. Of course, I could have done that. I could have made life hard for her. However, making life hard for her meant making life hard for Charles, and I already felt bad enough that I couldn't hold the whole thing together by myself. Obviously no one can make a relationship work by him or herself; even so, I had no choice but to try. I still wanted to see my son, and I also wanted to look good in the eyes of the court. Obviously, again, the court wouldn't have cared since I was about to agree to dumping money, as much as I possibly could, onto Cindi. But when you are the dad, you are already the underdog. Add to that how much of a selfish jerk I thought I was, and I could be convinced to do just about anything.

The next day when I got to work, there was another message from Kim. "Jesus," I thought, "What is wrong with this chick? This is enough from her. I will firmly tell her to knock it off." Then I opened the message.

> *John,*
>
> *Don't tell me to go out and meet guys. That is my business. The fact is, I met you, and I am emailing you. I am writing because I want to talk to you…not your situation or your problems…you. I am mad that you think I am just a silly girl after random guys. Maybe I shouldn't have kissed you, but I am glad I met you. I think you are a good person whether or not you are a guy, whether or not you want to date. I don't care about any of that. But don't think you are just going to say you can't drag people into this and do this by yourself. You don't have to respond to my emails, but I think you need someone to talk to and help you, and I am here when you do.*
> *Kim*

"Ugh!" I thought, "This girl just won't give up. She's a freaking stalker." So I decided to put a stop to this once and for all. She wasn't getting the picture, and I supposed I had to spell it out for her.

> *Kim,*
> *Look, I appreciate the sentiment, but there will be no more emails. Everyone I have talked to about this, I have stopped talking to. I have to do this on my own, so forget my talking to you or needing help. There is no help needed. I got myself into this, and I will get myself out. Enough.*
> *John*

I decided that was clear. Anyone with half a brain could see that I meant business. I mused that if she knew what a disaster, a lazy incompetent deadbeat I was, she would be running. Maybe this would give her the idea about how I really was.

In the meantime, my building projects were going well. Cindi already had her first client lined up for when her house was ready and when she was licensed. It was Jackie, the doula's new baby daughter. I was glad, at least, that she would have a friend visiting her every day. The two of them could talk about baby stuff just like in class the year before. They could talk about what a jerk I was for all I cared. I was just glad she would have someone else to talk to.

After she told me that, she also said that she planned to start up in December. When the daycare officially began, I would need to find another place to live. I had been there, living off of her long enough.

I would do anything for Charles, and the daycare did seem to be in his best interest: he could be home with his momma and also socialize with other kids. I reasoned, the daycare was something Cindi was excited about, and it would also keep her in check. You can't kill yourself in that circumstance or take off with everyone's kids. It might keep her sane, I figured, if she could keep it together.

A few days later, I got another email from Kim. I didn't reply. In fact, I didn't even open it. If she was looking for attention, I wouldn't even acknowledge the email. That would show her! I had had this happen before with a few girls who came to our shows. The girls always gave up eventually. This would be no different.

Still, I couldn't help but feel bad for her. She had seemed so nice. I really hated to be an ass to nice people. "Maybe I should apologize again," I thought. "No," I reasoned, "That would be just what she was looking for. I need to ignore this chick." Still, I wondered what she could have said in her email that had now been sitting there unread for a few days. Curiosity may have killed the cat, but it would not get the better of me! I was finally able to say I was going through my own problems completely on my own; unselfishly, hard-working, and with all the goodness I could muster. I may have been an awful person before, but I could change, I decided, by being good and not bothering others with my problems.

Days went by. Once in a while, the thought of that unopened email went through my head. Kim was such a cool person, and I was giving her the serious cold shoulder. And she'd brought Chronic a beer without asking anything in return. She was the kind of person I hoped to become, actually. I could learn a thing or two from this girl. I could take what I had seen and meld it into my own modus operandi. I would need to go over the emails again to gather all the clues I could about being a truly good person. Even a hint would suffice. I was selfish. She was unselfish. I needed to learn her secret.

Of course, once I saw how awful and self-centered I was in my emails versus how good she was in hers, the contrast was overwhelming. How could I be a good person if this was how I emailed a good person in return? How truly awful I was! And there, unopened, was the last email she had ever sent me. I had just shirked it like only a jerk like me would. Cindi was right about me: the most selfish person she knew. And I was...still! I was still swirling around this whirlpool unable to get out, no matter how hard I swam. Here I was thinking I would unselfishly get rid of this chick and the whole time I was being nothing but awful.

Of course! What I had been doing my whole life was the opposite of what I should have been doing. Perhaps if I decided, from now on, to do the exact opposite of what I initially decided, things would begin to turn around. I was a selfish jerk. Cindi had me pegged. All my decisions reflected it. From now on, the opposite decision would be made. I had initially decided not to open the email. That was before. Now it was time to do the opposite. So I opened it.

> *John,*
>
> *I get the picture. I will not talk about you or your problems. What you haven't given me a chance to say is that I would like your help. You are the dad of a small child, and you are a teacher. And you are a good teacher according to your students. I work in a daycare, and I want to teach preschool someday. I would like to pick your brain. I would appreciate hearing what you have to say about kids and education. Will you help me?*
>
> *Kim*

This seemed like a reasonable request, but there was only one problem. I was getting rid of everyone who knew anything about my situation with my divorce. My initial reaction was to not reply at all. She was trying to trick me into emailing her. So, yes, not replying was the decision. Therefore, according to my new decision-making routine, I *would* reply. I guessed hearing about what was on her mind would be fine, provided we didn't get into the subject of me. Replying suddenly seemed like a very kind thing to do. Maybe there was something to this doing the opposite of what I would normally do!

> *Kim,*

> *Sorry for the slow reply. I guess I wouldn't mind having my brain picked. What would you like to know?*
> *John*

This was short, sweet, and to the point, I thought. I could answer a few questions. Heck, I was trained in K-12 education. I probably knew a thing or two from sitting through all those boring classes. This might even be fun. I could look at my old textbooks and pull out some ideas from there. This was *helping* someone. I wanted nothing in return. This, I reasoned, was exactly what a good person would do. Now I was doing it! I could turn everything around. It was brilliant.

Someplace Fun

The next day I got my reply. Kim wanted to meet and ask her questions in person. Of course that was not going to happen, because I wanted nothing to do with anyone. But since not meeting was my natural reaction, I realized that I must do the opposite if I were to have any hope of getting out from under my "asshole" status. I could help someone. I could be a kind person. I would do this.

So I suggested lunch at a sandwich place. It was basically a business meeting. In fact, I made sure to emphasize that in my email. "You have to understand this is by no means a date. There will be *no kissing!*" I thought it was funny, but I also meant it. This was not a romance.

When we met up a few days later, we sat down and ate our sandwiches. I was ready to get down to business and then get out. That would satisfy my quota, I figured, for good behavior that day.

"So, what do you want to know, Kim?"

"Hmm? Oh, ok. Yes. Let's see..." She crossed her legs, leaned forward, and rested her chin on her fist very seriously. "Where did you grow up?"

"Um, in South Minneapolis. Two different neighborhoods, Armitage and Ericsson. Hey, they have mayonnaise packets? Cool." I opened one and squirted it on my sandwich.

"How was your childhood?"

"Ok, I see, you're establishing...ok. Is this for a paper, or what?"

"Sure."

"Oh, I see. 'Cause I'm an educator, huh?"

"And a dad."

"Right. Ok, well, you know...we had a busy neighborhood when I was a kid. Big Wheels everywhere. Kids playing kickball in the street after school. I think it was a lot of fun."

"Cool."

"Where did you grow up?" I asked.

"Iowa."

"Yeah? What are you doing up here?"

"I go to MCAD."

"Oh! Our drummer went to MCAD. Stephen Minister. Ever heard that name?"

"No, I don't think so."

"Doesn't matter. Before your time there, I guess."

"How old are you?"

"Me? 26. How old are you? Wait – scratch that. Not polite."

"22."

"Oh. I thought women didn't like to..."

"Why not?"

"I don't know. Anyway, what else?"

"Um, how long have you been teaching?"

"Gee. At the college?"

"Sure."

"Let's see...I started in September 2000. So I'm in my second year. Guess I haven't been there long."

"Do you like it?"

"This sandwich is great. How's yours?" I said with my mouth full.

"Oh, it's good! Wanna bite?" Her smile and quizzical face were adorable. Wait! That wasn't what this was about.

"No, no bites! That's like kissing! You're trying to trick me!"

"What? I am not! Come on," Her giggle was intoxicating.

"Wait! Back to the questions, dummy," I told myself. "This is flirting and I cannot do this." I redirected my thoughts. "Anyway, yeah, teaching's a lot of fun. God, the speech classes alone are a blast. You know, I convinced the college to let the students bring food and cook it in the classroom for their demonstration speeches. That cracked me up."

"That's funny!"

"They've had a strict no food policy for a long time. No water or anything in class. And last quarter a guy brought in a deep fryer."

"That's hilarious!"

"I don't know if anyone knew about that, but it was hilarious to me."

"You seem like you like to bend the rules."

"Yeah, once in a while, if it doesn't hurt anybody. The deep fryer didn't hurt anyone."

"No?" She laughed. "Good!"

I realized at that moment that this was fun. She was fun! But then I knew I couldn't have too much fun. This was supposed to be…I don't know…not fun.

"Anyway, I have to go pretty soon. Should we get to the serious questions?"

"Go? I have a lot more questions."

"Really?"

"I am writing a paper about you."

"Are you really writing a paper?"

"Sure! You don't believe me?"

"No, I believe you. You're learning to teach preschool, huh?"

"Someday. But I have to start preparing sometime, so I am using this as an excuse to start."

"Cool. Seriously though, I have to get going. I have a class in 40 minutes."

"Hmm…I do have a lot more questions."

"Email them to me."

"No, I like this way better. I get to see your personality. It will help me with filler for my paper if I need it."

"Well, I don't really know what to tell you."

"Tell me you can do this again."

"Uh, sure, I guess. Ok."

"Great!"

"But it's not a date."

"It won't be a date." Her smile washed over me again.

"Wanna come here again?"

"No, somewhere else."

"Gee, she's a little picky," I thought. "Ok, somewhere else. Where?"

"I don't know. Somewhere different. Someplace fun."

"Hey, that's bordering on date talk."

"No! Bordering on is not a date, is it?"

"Well, it could be. It *is* on the border. I don't want to go there."

"I *know!*" she giggled. She was enjoying this. I could not enjoy this…enjoyment would have been bad.

"Well, I think we should just come back here."

"No, we are not going to come back here."

"Then I guess we're done."

"Why?"

"Cause I don't want to have this turn into anything other than a Q and A."

"You can only 'A' here?"

"No, but I would prefer to."

"Are you going to help me or not?"

"I'm here aren't I?"

"Yes, and you can only be here. Hmph."

"That's right."

"Well that's stupid."

"What?"

"That's stupid. You are not being helpful at all." Wow, she sounded really disappointed. I wasn't being helpful? I looked away, out the window.

I had decided to only go to this sandwich shop. That was my final decision. That *was* my decision…my decision was to only go to the sandwich place, I mulled. But under my new process, I would only benefit by doing the opposite. So we would *not* come back to the sandwich place.

"Now you're not even talking? This is really helpful."

"Ok, here's the thing…"

"Ok."

"Normally I would refuse. But I'm trying to do the opposite of what I decide because I think I have been going wrong for a very long time."

"Ok?"

"So I decided that whatever my initial reaction would be, I would do the opposite."

"So we have a date!"

"No! We do not have a date! Jesus!" Her laugh was wonderful.

"I know! I'm kidding, John!" she laughed. I had to laugh, too. She was funny. If I could have placed it at that moment, her sense of humor would have been just a notch below her cute voice in terms of how alluring she was. Ah! I could not think like that!

"Well, this is tough to do. I don't think I want to do this anywhere else."

"But, since you would normally come back here…"

She was tricky!

"Ok, where should we go?"

"Somewhere fun."

"Fun?"

"Well, your idea was to go somewhere boring today."

"Yeah, this was my idea. Wait, you think this place is boring? Look at all the excitement. Look at that guy; he's eating the hell out of that sandwich. He's having a great time!"

"John! It's boring!" she giggled.

"Ok, fine. We'll do the opposite of boring. Where is somewhere fun to go? A playground?"

"No!" Her laugh was wonderful beyond words.

"No? Fine. Where?"

"You decide."

"Hmm…I have to decide?"

"Would you normally decide to go someplace fun with me?"

"No, not at all."

"So, do the opposite, and decide."

"Ok, but I will have to think about it for a day."

"That's fair. As long as you stick to your promise."

"Promise? What did I promise?"

"You promised to take me someplace fun!" Her smile was magnetic.

"Wait one second! This sounds like a date! I didn't want that!"

She sighed impatiently. "It's not a date, John!"

"Ok. Good. As long as it's not a date."

"Promise?"

"Promise it's not a date?"

"You don't have to promise that. You already have that ingrained in your head. You have to promise something else."

"I promise to *remind* you it's not a date."

"No!" She giggled. "You have to promise to take me someplace fun."

"And help you with your paper."

"And help me with my paper."

"Ok, I promise."

"Say the whole thing."

I just couldn't help but laugh. "I promise to take you somewhere fun to help you with your paper…"

"Good!"

"…And while doing so to remind you that it's not a date."

"Even better!" Her laugh was too much. I wanted to record it, so I could replay it whenever I needed it. At least, one more time, I would hear it again. I had promised, after all, to help her with her paper on a non-date someplace fun.

Losing the Battle

Nikki's Bar in Downtown Minneapolis used to be someplace fun to go. Cornbread Harris, the father of one of the most famous music producers, Jimmy Jam, was the blues pianist and singer who graced the bar twice a week with his raw gutbucket blues and jazz all night for the always-appreciative crowds. The piano, ragged and tucked under the staircase, would get to swinging pretty hard under his knowing fingers. The old 1970s Vocal Master PA system stashed behind the piano amplified the microphone which he hung around his neck with a metal coat hanger. The other musicians, usually an upright bass player, a drummer with only a snare and hi-hat, and a guitarist, crowded around Cornbread at the piano next to the staircase entrance, inches from the tables downstairs. Everything about the act was completely authentic, and he drew crowds like crazy.

When Cornbread wasn't playing, there was a solo piano guy who played jazz there. So I decided if we went on a night like that, it would be fun, but not too much fun – not "Cornbread" fun. And it would be quieter, so we could talk. It seemed like a good compromise to me. I set it up for the next weekend.

So as to avoid any trace of suspicion, I told Cindi I had a gig in some guy's basement that night. That would explain our band not being in the City Pages but would also explain my being out late. It was rather brilliant. Since we were separated, I suppose I didn't have to make excuses, but I never knew what would be used against me, so I made up an excuse anyway.

I told Kim in an email that we could just meet there, and she replied that the opposite of our meeting there would be my picking her up. This was getting a little out of my comfort zone, but I realized she was right, so I obliged. Actually, I thought, my truck would be a pretty good turn-off just in case. I had further worked on my tail pipe, but it still had a roar to it. For that matter, the truck itself was a bit of a rust bucket. I was sure she had guys in fancy cars picking her up, so this would one-down those guys. Anyone else she was seeing at the moment would be all the more alluring.

I held the tiny piece of paper with her address in my hand as it rounded the steering wheel, back and forth, while I tried to read it and watch for the building in between the dark of the streetlights. I passed her place a few times until I found a suitable parking spot on the street. It was a cold early November night, and I wanted to park somewhat close to the door. I got as close as I could and pulled into a spot on the street. Then I let the truck run and sat there for a half hour with my window open and the heater on. I was early, so I smoked six cigarettes while I waited. I was sure the cab would smell like smoke, but I decided it was for the better. You don't want to have a date that has a smelly truck. And my truck would be smelly, therefore making this evening *not a date!*

Finally, I could wait no more. I walked up to the building, double-checked the address, and looked up and down the little box for the name Kim. All I saw were last names. It was at that moment I realized I didn't know her last name! But, as luck would have it, someone was leaving the building and asked me if I wanted to come in.

"Yeah. I'm here to pick up Kim. Do you know her?"

"Sure. What's your name?" she asked.

"John."

"Oh!" She gave me a knowing look and her voice grew warmer. "Apartment 116. Right down there."

"Great. Thanks. Don't worry. I'm not here to steal anything!"

"I know," she said.

"How could she know?" I wondered.

I walked down to 116. The carpet in the hall was filthy. The walls were awful. It wasn't like it was a dump necessarily, but the yellowed, slightly dirty paint along with the matted, worn-looking carpet, dulled and frayed with time, left much to be desired. But it made sense that students would live here. It was a minor step up from dorms.

I knocked on the door, and Kim answered shortly after with a flat iron in her hand.

"You're here. Who let you in?" She sounded out of breath.

"I don't know. Some girl."

"Oh, my roommate!"

"She seemed to know who I was."

"Yes! Have a seat. I am almost ready."

"Sure."

"Here's the remote." She moved swiftly.

"Ok." I sat on her couch. It wasn't bad. It looked secondhand but was comfortable enough. I had no interest in TV. I just wanted to get going. I was becoming uncomfortable. I had gotten myself into a weird situation in this step-up-from-a-dorm-room in which I sat. Essentially, I was hanging out with a student. Not a student at my college, but still, a student. The college hated that. It was disconcerting. I had always avoided situations like these. It was a major offense for faculty to get romantically involved with a student. And this situation, my sitting in a student's living room, seemed to be teetering on that offense, no matter how innocent. Still, she was a student at another college, not mine. She was also about to graduate. Even so, I was uncomfortable. I wrestled with myself.

Kim went into what I assumed was the bathroom to finish with her hair. It felt like a date. Actually, it really felt like a date. Should I say something? Should I back out? But it felt good too. For the first time in a long time, it felt like I wasn't the underdog. It had been a bit like that with Cindi, but at the time I had not been a teacher. I was on minimum wage, barely getting by. And I was a musician. Cindi hated those things about me. She brought them up often.

Yet to Kim, I was the same guy who she'd met at Scott Youngstead's party. I was an underground musician who also was an English Professor, and she seemed to perceive both as positives. It struck me that out of all the guys she had to choose from, not only was I a long shot to her, but I was also worth the effort she was making. I was alluring as hell. However, I had a dark past. Wait, chicks love that kind of stuff! I was either sitting on her secondhand couch imagining how interesting I was to her, or I actually was that interesting to her. I wasn't quite sure which it was, though. What I did know was this could become very dangerous very quickly.

I sat there on the couch and looked around the room. Kim had funny pictures of herself by the TV. In one, she was riding a toy horse and laughing. It was funny, although not flattering. But she had a sense of humor. That was flattering. The kitchen was small and adjoined the living room. It was clean except for burn marks on the counter. Who knew what had gone on in this place since the building had been built?

Then she came out wearing a slightly oversized gray sweatshirt that had a large V crudely cut in the neck. It made the sweatshirt hang askew off her shoulder. It was unusual and completely gorgeous. She had makeup on. That scared and excited me. "Ready?" she asked.

I just sat there and looked. This was a date. This was a second date, in fact. She looked nervous.

"What?" she asked, breathless.

"I, um…wow."

"Wow?"

"Are you…You look…"

"Is this ok? I don't even know where we are going. Should I change?"

"Do *not* change," I said, my eyes fixed on her.

"What?" she asked self-consciously.

"Nothing. Just don't change."

"Fine. I'm not changing. Should we go? What are you looking at?" She bit her bottom lip and looked down at her clothes. She was jittery.

"I'm looking at you."

"Well stop it. Let's go."

"Sorry. Yeah, let's go."

Suddenly, I cared how the truck smelled. Actually, I became quite jittery, myself. We went out into the cold night and walked to my truck. I held her hand while she crossed over an icy spot on the sidewalk.

"Here's your truck! Good! Where's the rum? In back?" She giggled, and her smile complimented her sexy cheek bones. I opened her door.

"No rum back there. Sorry."

"I think I want some rum again," she said as she climbed in.

"The rum is on me tonight." I closed the door, went around to mine, and fumbled with the key.

She reached over, pulled on the handle, and the door opened.

"You've been smoking."

"Sorry about that."

"I don't care. I love your truck."

I had forgotten. We had been at my truck the night we met. We had a good memory associated with it. The truck would not one-down any other guy. "It runs pretty good," I said, trying to avoid what I was thinking. She did love my truck. It was my truck, but just a little of it was already hers. We both knew it. The one thing I owned belonged partially to a really cool girl. It was an exciting thought.

"Where are we going?"

"Oh, I never told you where I wanted to go."

"No, you didn't."

I backed up and pulled out of the space. "I wonder why I didn't."

"Have you decided?"

"Well, that depends," I teased as I stopped at the light on Lake Street.

"It depends? Do I get a choice?"

"No."

She giggled, "Ok. Then where are we going?"

"I have no idea. I don't even know where we are."

"Are you kidding?"

"Do I sound like I'm kidding?"

"Are you teasing me?" Suddenly her voice rose. "John! This is a one-way! What are you *doing?*"

"Oops! Too late! Hang on!" I sped the wrong way down the one way street.

"Are you drunk?"

I laughed nervously at the embarrassment of having just done something completely stupid and dangerous in front of Kim. This could end up like Maggie all over again, I realized. I was going to change my mind about her, and then she would change her mind about me.

"No, not drunk. Just stupid, I guess."

"Do you know where we are going for real?"

"Well, now I'm really not sure. I might drive us off a cliff if I'm not careful!"

"Stop it!" she laughed. There was that magical aural salve I desperately needed: her laugh. I wished I could keep it. I had wished for it so many times. Maybe I would, I decided, be able to keep it. It was a wonderful thought. Just for a moment, I let myself believe I could.

"John! *Stop!*" The light was red, and I just sailed right through.

"You *are* drunk!"

"I'm really not. I don't know what is wrong with me! I'm so sorry. I should be keeping you safe. I am sorry, Kim."

She laughed nervously. "Just pay attention."

"I will. I don't know what's wrong with me," I repeated. "I never drive like this."

"Are you distracted for some reason?"

"I can't say."

"You're diiis-traaac-ted!" she sang mockingly.

"Stop distracting me!"

She laughed again. "I'm diiis-trac-ting you!" she sang again.

"Do you want to live or die, Kim?"

"I'm enjoying living right now, thank you very much!"

"Ok, stop distracting me."

"Where are we going?"

"Downtown!"

"Where?"

"You'll see."

"Tell me!"

"No!"

"Why not?"

"Cause it's more fun to not tell you." I smiled, watching the road very carefully.

"Your driving is improving. I'm sooo impressed!" she mocked.

"You ain't seen nothin' yet."

"Oh good!" she laughed. "I thought this was how you always drove!"

"Well, I guess it is when I'm distracted."

"What is distracting you?"

"You are! Now stop!"

"Hmmm hmm-hmm hmmm hmmmmmmmm," she hummed her little mocking song quietly.

We eventually pulled into the lot across from Nikki's.

It was crowded inside. The jazz pianist ended his first set as we arrived, and he went on break.

"*This* looks fun!" she announced as we walked in. Heads turned to follow Kim as the greeter led us to the overflow room. The guys looking at her pissed me off.

Then we just started talking. I don't really remember about what. I just remember we talked and talked. It was so comfortable…so truly good…so wonderful. I tried with all my might not to stare into the huge V in her sweatshirt's neckline. When she leaned towards me, I knew heaven was inside that sweatshirt. I wrestled with my feelings, wrestled my eyes away, but I was wearing down. I was losing the battle with myself.

Kim was beyond anything I could have wished for. Her eyes: so sensual. Her lips…I knew how soft. She was so happy, so glad to be with me. Her smile was the cleanest, most abundant water in the driest desert. She was so smart and so funny. So sure of herself. I almost could not believe it. It was so hard to convince myself that I was actually there. I had fallen into heaven and was thinking I might just stay. The paradise from which I'd pulled myself in October was still there, waiting. I had gone back to find it even more wonderful than it had seemed at first visit.

"How come you aren't telling me this is not a date?" she asked. "You promised!" she giggled. She knew. She could see it all over my face. She was winning. She was accomplishing what she had set out to do. She nearly had me. She became more and more confident throughout the night because of it. She was relishing this turn of events. Her gamble was paying off. What could I do? I was mesmerized.

"How come what?"

"You *promised* to remind me that this wasn't a date. When are you going to do what you promised?" Her fake sad eyes mocked me.

"I don't know." She had me. Goddamn it, she had me.

"You promised," she pouted. My insides were jelly. I couldn't tell her that. I wanted to grab onto her and never let go. I couldn't say it wasn't a date.

"I just…I was going to…"

"Wait, what are you trying to do?" she teased.

"Nothing." I didn't want to mess anything up, even if she was teasing.

"Are you trying to go back on your promise?"

I smiled. "Well…"

"John! Is this a date? Answer me this instant!" she chided.

How could I answer? I felt caught between what I wanted and what I…I didn't even know what; some enigmatic thing that I was supposed to do, if only I could remember it.

"You've become very quiet," she sang. "What's going on with you?"

"I just don't want to talk about it."

"You have to answer me, Johnny," she sang again.

"No. I can't."

She leaned across the table. "We're on a daaaate," she sang quietly, up close to my ear so that only I could hear her say it. And then I looked. I looked into heaven, into the V in her shirt, and swallowed hard; a darkened heaven, only slightly visible, awaited. I shivered. Oh my God, I thought, I have died and am now in a place even better than heaven. Thank you! Thank you! Wait, I was dreaming, I thought. "I can't wake up," I told myself. "I have to stay in this dream as long as I can."

She sat back down and smiled. "Your face is flushed. I wonder why…?"

I smiled and looked down shyly.

"Do you want to go?"

"No."

"But we have to."

I was completely spaced out of my head. "We do?"

"They're going to close."

"Already?"

She leaned across the table again and brushed her lips against my ear, so I could feel her warm, tickly breath. "You like me, Johnny!"

She sat back down. I shivered again. I took a half-breath. "You're right," I said quietly, almost unable to say the words.

"Come on, let's get out of here!"

"Ok." I stood up.

"Hey wait, silly. We have to pay."

"Oh yeah! I don't know what's wrong with my brain!" I sat down.

"You're disss-traaaac-ted!" she sang again.

"You're distracting me," I said, looking down at the table.

"I know," she sighed knowingly.

Later, when we got back to her place, she asked me in.

"I better not."

"But I want you to," she pouted.

"I do too, but I have to go back." I swallowed hard. I had to go back to the hell from where I had come. My insides dropped out of me onto the floor of the cab. The hollow shell which was me had to go back to sleep in the hellish abyss.

"Why do you live there?"

"I can't live there much longer. I am getting kicked out. I don't know anymore, really, why I live there. I was trying to protect Charles. Maybe I'm just making things worse. I don't know."

"You look sad."

"Yeah."

"It will work out. I will help you."

"You will?"

"Yes. You like me, Johnny. And I like you. I am here to help you. Will you let me?"

"Yes."

"Is this a date?"

"Yes."

"How do you know?"

"Cause I want to kiss you."

"I thought you couldn't."

"I don't care. I want to."

"Then do."

Her lips were soft and comfortable. The sectional couch, when I got home, was hard and worn flat. I hated it. I hated myself for sleeping on it, hated myself for losing my family. Hated that I rubbed my own nose in it every night.

In my truck was everything I owned. Part of that truck even belonged to Kim. Part of it was hers. I relished the thought. None of it was Cindi's. I sat up and pulled my pillow onto my lap. The pain of this horrid existence, contrasted with my brief night of heaven, was unbearable. I went back out to my truck. Kim had just been sitting on the seat next to me. Where was she now? I had dropped heaven off and had gone straight to hell. I couldn't be on that couch anymore. I had to go. It utterly repulsed me. Here in this house, I was the festering corpse of who I could never be: a good husband to Cindi. Every night I had lain in this nightmarish hell in the rotting stench of my failure while heaven was so close by that if I dared to, I could touch it.

I looked back at the house I had once enthusiastically called home. I had lost everything inside. My truck roared to a start.

An Ending and a Beginning

It occurred to me as I drove west on I-94 that endings and beginnings were again overlapping. I had seen this phenomenon when Charles was born and when my great-grandmother died shortly after. It felt to me at the time that I was repeating the pattern: allowing a negative person to hurt the family. But I was choosing another road at the moment. I was choosing to walk away.

"Pa, why didn't you just leave her?"

"Son, I married her for better or for worse. For better or for worse."

Was my changing course well advised? Was leaving my son with Cindi without my watchful eye a good idea? Would she settle down and stay in check with the opening of the daycare and other people's kids in the house? Should I say something to these people who were about to trust Cindi with their small children? Would they believe me? Would I further jeopardize my relationship with Charles? These questions plagued me as I drove away.

If there were some connection between birth and death, could there be some connection between the birth and death of a relationship? Were we meant to burn through relationships when they no longer were of use, when we in the relationship no longer saw eye-to-eye? Were we meant, once we had used that person and had gotten what we could, to throw the friendship away – to leave it on the roadside? Or were we meant to go back again and again, horrible as it was, medicating ourselves with Bromo-Seltzer, alcohol, food, and anything else that worked in order to fulfill a promise, regardless of how ill-advised and uninformed the decision? Could the course be changed, or would the new road eventually lead back to the old?

Were we repeating patterns, driving the same old roads, because we were not only missing the signs telling us to use caution but also because the signs were illegible? Were we even capable of conceiving a better course, one that would not lead back to the old? Would Cindi and I go at it for the next 18 years (or more) because the nature of the relationship, with its binding decision, the baby, meant that we could never evolve from our differences to a better place? Could we even work together to pursue a course to that place? And what of the baby who would grow into a man? What would this relationship teach him?

The lights from the moderately vacant Downtown Minneapolis flashed by as I glanced at them driving I-94 back into Minneapolis. The dull sound coming from the fault line in my exhaust pipe growled beneath me. I was driving to Roland's house to take him up on his offer of a spare room for a few days. Maybe a week. I had no idea what lay ahead. But I knew the road there and knew my own way in through the side door. I knew I could have a place to sleep somewhat indefinitely. The questions plaguing me would have to wait. I was tired and beaten. I needed to sleep.

And I slept. On the bare mattress with only my pillow. It was an uncomfortable sleep, but sleep nonetheless. Whenever I awoke in the darkness, I replayed Kim's words: "You like me, Johnny. And I like you. I am here to help you." They were my nightlight. I could fall back asleep knowing she was there. I suppose I had lost the fight in trying to solve my problems alone, but it was such a pleasant thought that I had someone backing me. Beat up as I was, I had someone who would clean my wounds, revive me, and give me a moment to regain my strength before going back into the ring. I hoped, anyway.

I was put up in Roland's spare room until I could find a place to live. While I arranged that, I also asked to see Kim again the next weekend. Unfortunately, she had to study. Sensing my disappointment, she offered a compromise. I could come over and hang out while she studied. It reminded me of where I had been in my relationship with Maggie once I had convinced her to go out with me again. Sadly, by time I did that and she realized she also wanted to pursue a relationship, it was almost finals week. We wanted nothing more than to curl up in a bed all day and look at each other, kiss, and snuggle: all the stuff you try to do while you're deciding whether or not you both really want to have a relationship.

Finals had made that lazy dream impossible for Maggie and me, so we'd made a pact: we would study together, so we could constantly be together. But we *had* to study. No talking, no gazing into each other's eyes, no kissing, only looking at our books. Still, we glanced up once in a while, just to smile or blow a kiss to each other. It was so hard, we had to admit, to just sit there and only communicate a very little bit.

Once in a while we caught ourselves talking. We would joke and laugh and say how much we liked each other. Then we would realize what we were doing and say, "Our Agreement!" like it was our secret law. All the while, we were proving not only that we could control ourselves, as not to jeopardize each other's grades, but also how much we were actually falling in love, as we couldn't help but talk to each other. We were so contented to be together no matter what the circumstance. The mutual self-denial created a kind of magnetic force between us. Thinking of that circumstance, so early in that relationship, reminded me to take it slow and not over-do it with Kim.

When I got to Kim's on Friday night, I was led into her bedroom.

"You don't study in the living room?"

"No, I study right here." Her books and drawings were on a desk at one end of the room. Her bed was against the adjacent wall, and the TV was at the other end. The only other things in the room were a closet and a dresser, both on the fourth wall across from the bed.

"You can watch TV while I study. I won't mind."

There I was, suddenly and unexpectedly, with a permit to her bedroom. During most of my third dates, I tended to steer clear of the bedroom. I didn't want things to start out, third date or not, with my trying to get into the bedroom. It seemed to give the wrong impression, I thought, about what I wanted the relationship to be focused on.

That's a pretty un-guy thing to say, and obviously it sounds fake, but I had truly always been looking for a long-term relationship. Most guys, I guess, are looking for sex while in their twenties, and sex appealed to me then as well. But for some reason, I knew a stable relationship would not only bring sex, but more meaningful sex because I would be with someone I truly loved and admired. That always seemed like the way to go, despite hearing the exploit stories that I undoubtedly heard from my buddies in college and later in the band. Again, I was probably the lamest guy I knew, but that's the way I've always been.

Even so, her bedroom was a thrilling elixir. I sat on her bed (against some pillows she found and propped up for me like a cozy chair), put on the Vikings' game, and rooted along as she sat behind me and studied. But her studying was drawing, so it didn't seem much like studying to me. Still, she was so intent, so focused. I wondered if she was even aware I was in the room.

But once in a while, during the commercials, I would look over and just take in the scene. Then she would glance over and say, "Are you staring at me?"

"Yes," I would answer.

And she would say, "Stop it. You're making me uncomfortable!"

And I would say, "I can't help it."

She would shyly turn back to her desk, then look at me again, and say, "Stop!"

I know I could have stopped, but I didn't want to. I wanted to soak up the situation in which I found myself. Here I was, drinking the Rum and Coke she had bought and mixed for me, lounging on her bed in her room, and watching football. All the while, the most wonderful girl I could possibly fathom was sitting behind me, and I could look at her anytime I wanted. There was no way I would not look at her. Looking at her made me float in mid-air, no matter how much she protested.

When she did, I told her all this. She was letting it sink in, too; my being there. My existence. My beginning to belong to her. I wasn't going anywhere, and she didn't seem to be either.

When she finished studying, she lay on her stomach on the side of her bed and looked up at me, her chin in her hands.

"What are *you* looking at?"

"I'm staring at you, so you can see how it feels!" She smiled.

"I'm used to girls staring at me."

"Come on!"

"When you're gorgeous like I am, everyone stares."

"You think you're that gorgeous?"

"Duh! Are you disagreeing?"

"No." She smiled again.

"You think I'm goooor-geous!" I singingly mocked.

"John!" she protested.

"Well, you do."

"I do not." she giggled.

I swung my legs over her. "Then I can take my business elsewhere."

"Hey!" She grabbed my leg. "I want your business to stay right here!" She laughed.

"What?" I raised an eyebrow.

"I didn't mean it like that, you butt!" She was cracking herself up. That was a good sign.

"Guess what?" I asked.

"What?"

"I'm living at Roland's house now."

"You are? Your guitar player?"

"Yep."

"You left?"

"Well, it was either that or be thrown out by a judge."

"That's great!"

"Think so?"

"Yes! John, that's awesome!"

"Why?"

"Cause it is!"

"I guess. The only problem is: we're still married."

"I know. You won't even take off your ring."

"Because I'm married."

"To a bitch. And you said you were separated."

"We are, but I still made a promise. She can throw me out, but the promise was made."

"You made a promise to a bitch who abuses you."

"I can't prove that."

"So it never happened?"

"No, it happened, all right. It's happening now."

"The court can think whatever it wants. It doesn't make the court right."

"Well, they haven't decided anything yet."

"So there you go," she said.

"So I'm still married. And does the dissolution of the marriage necessarily dissolve the promise?"

"What was the promise?"

"I promised her I would make it work. I promised I would help with the baby."

"You can do that when you're divorced."

"But not in the same way."

"Has she given you that choice?"

"No, I have no choice at all."

"So you have to do the best you can within the situation. You can't change her."

"But I have to work with her."

"So get a divorce and work with her as it pertains to Charles. I will help you."

"Yeah?"

"I like you, Johnny."

"I like you, Kim."

"So we will help each other."

It dawned on me at that moment that Kim would always be like that. She was like that in her twenties, she would be like that in her thirties, and on from there. I had this flash of memory of walking with Emily. She'd said she had always been the way she was. The way I liked her. I had been looking for my version of Emily, and it sure as hell had not been Cindi. However, three gigs until the end of the band's life, I had finally found someone with the qualities I admired in Emily. It was then that I realized I had better not mess this up, and I had better not overstay my welcome.

"Ok. I better go."

"Go? Go where?"

"Home."

"Why?"

"I can't stay here."

"Why not?"

"I just can't."

"Fine."

"Kim, I can't stay here, and you know it."

"I don't know it."
"Well I do."
"You're mean."
"I'm sorry, but we're just not there yet."
"Fine. I didn't say we were."
"Ok, good. See? I'm right."
"Fine."
I went back to Roland's.
The next day, I sent Kim an email.

> Kim,
> I hope you're not mad I left last night, but I just felt I could not stay. I hope you understand.
> John

I didn't get a reply. No email, no call, nothing. Days went by, and I wondered what had happened. Had I blown it completely by not staying at her apartment that night, so soon into our relationship?

Still, I stood by my decision. I was not going to have that kind of relationship. I didn't care how awesome Kim was; I was doing relationships at a reasonable speed from now on. No matter how alluring, how sweet, how right and wonderful she was, I would not rush things. She wanted to rush? She could rush with somebody else.

I sat in my free room at Roland's on the mattress on the floor. I sat with my feet on the floor and my elbows on my legs, bent forward. Some enchanting guy I was. I was homeless, unable to keep a girl, and nothing but a shitty dad. What did I deserve? A mattress and a 12" TV on a floor seemed about right for me. College professor? Huh! Underground musician? Bullshit! I was a loser. I had lost everything, and that's what a loser does. An ending and a beginning? Yeah, right. This was two endings. Whatever Kim thought she saw, it did not exist, and she knew it. The night came and went, and I didn't care.

CD Release Party

Date: Thu Nov 8, 2001, 1:07 pm
Subject: CD Release @ The Cabooze Nov 20

We are excited to announce the release of our new CD and our very special party to celebrate!
    When? Friday, November 20th, 2001 -- show starts at 8:30
    Where? The Cabooze in Minneapolis; 917 Cedar Ave., off of Cedar and Franklin next to Whiskey Junction and The Joint
    Who? Us and our friends!
    Why? It's time to have a huge-ass party
    How? With the assistance of music, booze, friends and family

Hey, we hope to see you all there. Thanks for being patient and hanging with us during the production of the CD. We think you will find it worth the wait! Come celebrate with us a week from Friday.
    See ya then!

I heard about some stuck-up musician walking out of the Cabooze because it seemed like a dive to him, but I thought it was a damn good bar. Not a stadium, not a trendy club, but a bar. Black walls with little decor. Warn seats and old pool tables. The room was long and narrow with a bar at each end. The stage was in the middle of one of the long walls. There were pool tables and a foosball table. I guess, at worst, the place was utilitarian. Still, the stage was big and fairly deep, and the on-stage sound was usually great for us. The only place that was better to play in the Twin Cities, in my opinion, was the Main Stage at First Avenue. The room at The Cabooze was somewhat smaller, but it was still a great hangout. It wasn't a corny, silly looking club with flashing lights and neon. It was a band's bar. People came to listen to live music first and foremost. If you could pack the room, your band was doing pretty well. A thousand people is nothing to sneeze at.

And it was packed by time the first band went on at 8:30, and only became more so as the night progressed. I sat in the back room, smoking and listening to the show going on outside the walls. I would peek my head around the corner once in a while and motion for another Rum & Coke from Troy the bartender. Then I would slink back to the green room and smoke and drink some more. I was beginning to hate all the people. Beginning to hate being an attraction. Beginning to hate people coming up to me like they knew me and wanting to talk about unimportant crap. Beginning to hate all the girls I saw.

Elizabeth was there. I remember that. I avoided her. No more Elizabeths. No more Kims and Cindis. No more, period. I was to do the show and then go back to my mattress on the floor. That was my life. Eventually, I would end up in a courtroom and be given my sentence: a lifetime in hell. What did any of it matter?

We were on at 11 PM after the second band. We played 45 minutes and then took a 15 minute break. I always hated taking a break that late in the night because people would inevitably leave. But that night, when we got back up to do our second set, it looked as if even more people had come. The CDs were flying out the door, too. We brought the entire 1000 from our first and only pressing, and we found out at the break that almost 500 had already sold. This was a big event. And I didn't care.

We started playing the intro of one of the first songs the band ever did to salute all the die-hard fans that started out with us in 1996. Everyone was so amped up after hearing a tune we hadn't played in years, that the rest of the night was the wildest celebration I can remember seeing at the Cabooze. Every song we did made the crowd go wilder.

The wilder they went, the more dancing and general drunkenness there was. The area in front of the stage was a solid, gyrating mass of people. I remember getting flashed for only the second time in the band's history by some girl in the audience that night. We knew we were having a good show by the time that happened.

I stood there and continued to look at the crowd, more entertained by them, really, than by what we were doing. As I looked down, right in front of me was Kim and some other girl I had never seen before. They were talking when I looked at them. Then Kim noticed that I had seen her; she waved and smiled.

"Great. Now what?" I thought.

By the time the show ended, she was gone. I looked at the whole bar full of people filing out. Kim was nowhere to be seen. "Well, I guess that was that," I said to myself as I put away my stuff. We hung around for a while, taking care of the rest of the CDs, T-shirts, and general band accumulation while chatting with the bartenders. They had had a great night.

Finally, I made my way into the cold night behind the bar. A whoosh of iciness whacked me in the face as I walked out from the hot sweatiness of the Cabooze. The wind had picked up considerably and had a good bite to it. I kept my head down; my eyes watered at the punishing air as I made my way to my truck. I could see from a couple of quick glances that the back alley had cleared out enough that I would now be able to get out. I opened up the tailgate and slid in the Rhodes, its stand, and my dolly.

As I closed the back, I heard a girl's voice.

"Hi!"

I didn't want to know who it was. I turned around, and there was Kim all bundled up in her brown parka. She shivered but a smile crossed her face.

"You're here," I said. "Did you know I would be here?"

"Of course."

"You did?"

"Yes!"

"Oh."

"I came to see you!"

"Ok. Why are you in the back alley?"

"I saw your truck." Her friend was in the car on the other side of the street. She waved at me.

"Who's that?"

"She's my friend. We go to school together."

"You rode with her?"

"Yeah." She walked closer to me, shivering. "I liked your show."

"Yeah?"

"Yeah."

"I didn't know you were coming."

"Of course I would."

"You never responded to my email."

"I was mad at you."

"Are you still mad?"

"No. I will never stay mad at you."

"You won't?"

She walked up to me. "Never."

"Why?"

"'Cause. I like you."

"You like me?"

She put her lips to my ear like she had at Nikki's. "I really like you, John."

I don't know what made me say it, but almost as a reflex I quietly said, "I want to go to your apartment." I didn't want to. That is, I hadn't wanted to until just then.

Her lips left my ear and found my lips. She was so wonderful. She stopped and looked into my eyes, a little softer and slightly sad. "Drive me home."

I couldn't refuse. Not this time.

Away from the Edge

I was careful that we didn't have sex that night. I didn't want to go there. But we slept close to each other. It was an amazing feeling, to be pressed close against her skin. She was so soft. We were on the verge of a new evolution in our relationship. The next day, we had nothing to do. We made food and watched movies. No finals, no work, just time. All she wore was an oversized sweatshirt.

When I found out she couldn't use one side of her kitchen sink because the drain leaked terribly and the maintenance guy was taking forever to get to it, I went out and bought a few tools and a new piece of PVC. Whoever had installed the P trap under the sink didn't bother to cut one of the pipes to the right length, and over time it had pulled away at the joint. With some better measuring and a new gasket, everything fit together as it should have, and both sides of the sink could again be used.

It wasn't that she was awed by my ability to measure, cut, and reinstall a piece of plastic; but I think it was a very comfortable-feeling event for her. Her dad was a mechanic, and Kim was used to seeing the man in her life fixing things like I had just done. She was all smiles and compliments the whole time I worked, yet she was experienced enough that she wasn't on top of me while I worked.

Thanksgiving came too soon to meet her family. We weren't quite to that point in the relationship. I really wasn't sure I wanted to get to that point yet, either. So she went home to Iowa, and I went home to my folks' for Thanksgiving. However, my entire family was in Milwaukee with my grandparents. I didn't really have the money or the vehicle to make the trip, so my mom had left me a frozen turkey pot pie, and I ate it by myself at their dining room table on Thanksgiving night. All I had to be thankful for was Kim, a girl who was far away at that moment. That really got me to thinking as I sat at the piano in the basement after eating my solo dinner.

I plunked out some chords, scratched out some quick lyrics, and rehearsed until I got the song to where I liked it. Then I called

Kim's cell phone, got the voice mail as I knew her parents' house was out of range, and recorded about eight takes until I was satisfied. I used the voicemail function that allowed me to discard the message when I heard it and didn't like the take. It was pretty much like being in the studio. I worked on it for about an hour until I got a take with which I was satisfied, and then I submitted it to her voicemail. I never recorded it except to her phone. The results were better than I expected.

Kim called me later, so excited and happy that I had left her a song as a message. She had already listened to it several times from somewhere in range of a cell phone tower. Years later, I would learn that she played that song every night I wasn't with her before she went to bed.

When she called from wherever she got a signal, she was breathless on the phone; just like she had been the night I first went to her apartment.

"Where are you?" she asked.

"At my folks'."

"Did you have a good dinner?"

"Yeah. Frozen turkey pot pie!" I laughed. It was pretty funny, really.

"What? That's what your mom made?"

"Well, she left it for me. No one is here. They're all in Milwaukee."

"What?"

"It's just me. Thanksgiving feast for one."

"I should have invited you here!"

"I don't know that we're quite there yet."

"Ok."

Silence.

"Anyway, I liked your song."

"It's your song. I sang it for you."

"I liked *my* song then." She giggled. It was not a bad Thanksgiving at all, because I could hear her cute giggle.

"Why don't you come down here?"

"Ha! No, I just don't...how would we explain that?"

"I don't know."

"Here's the guy I'm kinda going out with?"

"And he's married to someone else!"

"Exactly."

"I could say you are my boyfriend. You're my friend, and you're a boy."

"But that doesn't make me your boyfriend."

"No? Maybe it does."

"Well, let's think about that. How many boys are you friends with?"

"A few."

"So you have a few boyfriends."

"No, not like that."

"Like what?"

"Not like this. Not like you."

"You want me to be your boyfriend?"

"No!"

"Ok then."

"Maybe," she giggled.

"No *and* maybe? You're trying to trick me!"

"No!" she laughed.

"I'm not that great of a candidate, really. No one even wants to have Thanksgiving dinner with me!"

She laughed. "I do! Well, I do now."

"Great...after it's too late."

"Yeah!" Her laugh was incredible.

"Well, maybe we should think about this. If I were your boyfriend, that would make you my girlfriend, and I'm not sure that's too great for you either."

"Why not?"

"Hm. That *would* be pretty great for you, actually. I see where you're coming from."

"John!"

I was starting to enjoy making that beautiful laugh happen whenever I wanted. "I don't know. Can we actually do this over the phone?"

"No, you should come here."

"Actually, I would like to. I do have to spend tomorrow with Charles, though."

"Bring him!"

"No. I would be taking him out of state, and I could get in all kinds of trouble for that."

"Then I will come to you."

"Huh?"

"I'll be there tomorrow after you see Charles. What time?"

"I don't know. Five?"

"Come to my apartment at six."

By time I got there, Kim had already been to the store and picked up a few things for me. I was being nurtured, and it felt incredible. She had a toothbrush, a towel, a special cocktail glass for Rum & Coke, and a pillow. I was allowed to stay there whenever I wanted. All I had to do was agree to be her boyfriend. It actually reminded me of the joke about what you call a keyboardist without a girlfriend: homeless. I wanted it so bad despite the truth to that joke. I wanted to belong to her. But there would always be the conflict. I was adored on one hand and loathed and degraded on the other. I would always be on the edge, looking down into the cesspool, the place I belonged. But how could I say no? I had to admit it to her…had to admit that I loved her. There was no question.

She knew. And I knew she loved me. We really were crazy about each other. It was nice just to be able to come out and say it. It was when we had that conversation that I was told more:

"I told my family about you."

"What?"

"What's wrong?"

"Good Lord, Kim! I'm still married! What will they think?"

"Only my sister knows that part."

"Jesus."

"No, she understands. She thinks you are good for me."

"She doesn't know me then, does she?"

"You *are* good for me."

"Yeah, how?"

"You are a great guy. You are a wonderful dad. You must see that."

"I'm not your dad, so what's the difference? And I'm not a wonderful dad."

"Well, not according to Cindi. But she's crazy!"

"That's the only person who matters."

"She doesn't matter. I do, and I want a boyfriend who I know is capable of being a great dad."

"Uh! I really don't want kids, hon."

"You called me hon? Aw…"

"Seriously."

"I know you don't right now."

"No, I don't."

"Fine. Still, you don't know what a good dad you are? Really?"

"Hm."

"Why else would you deal with all the shit you are dealing with? You're a good dad!"

"Hm."

"You must see it. You're an incredible guy. That's why I love you."

"But I don't deserve this. I don't know what I am doing!" I was becoming angry. "I shouldn't be here! What the fuck am I doing?"

"Hey, it's ok." Kim stood up and backed away.

"No, it's not!" The anger was rising. I stood up ready to fight an invisible enemy: my conflicted emotions. My breathing quickened.

"John! That's enough! Sit down right now." She was backing out the door of her room.

Every muscle contracted. I sat on the bed again and punched my leg.

"Breathe," she said quietly and emphatically. I tried. "Shhhh…" she said, coming closer again.

She stood near me as I wrestled with my adrenalin. "I hate this!"

"I know. Shhhh…"

I began to calm down a bit. "It's hard for me, all of this."

"So let me make it easy. Come on, I need your help."

She took my hand and led me to the shower. She needed someone to wash her back. She couldn't think of anyone else she would want to do it. It completely calmed me. She was so beautiful. It was so nice to just be there, both of us absorbed in each other, naked, and enjoying our becoming closer. My anger melted away.

Still wet from the shower, we fell onto her bed, completely absorbed, completely entangled. I remember crying afterward. I felt so guilty for being so well treated and loved. I knew I did not deserve it. I knew what Kim could not see: who I really was. I knew I should not have been allowed this pleasure. The tears fell onto her neck, and she held me tight with her arms and her legs, pulling a blanket over the both of us. I nuzzled up to the smell of shampoo and conditioner in her wet hair.

"I know. I know," she whispered. "It's not so bad. You stay with me, and you'll see. It's not so bad. Shhhh."

It was nurturing I had not earned. It was given without expectation. And it was wonderful and healing, yet I knew I should not accept it.

"Shhhh. I know, baby." Her sweet voice in my ear was pulling me, very slowly, away from the edge. "Shhhh. I'm right here, baby. Shhhhh."

Crap in Paradise

As wonderful as my time with Kim was that December, Cindi was an ever-present jagged edge, protruding and ready to find me. She called almost every day with something I had to do. It was home improvement stuff for the daycare, or she wanted me to take this or that box of my stuff. She needed me to go to the doctor with Charles or called me to calm him down. I would sing to him on the phone. Then she would cuss me out, screaming that I was a deadbeat dad.

"Why are you doing this to me?" She would ask. I didn't have an answer. I never understood why she was mad. Always, there existed this nagging, painful threat behind me, always on my back. If I disagreed with anything she said, she would scream through the phone and tell me I would never see Charles again.

The person who doesn't care has all the power. I thought Charles needed to have a dad. That was my perspective. From hers, a dad was not necessary. I wanted him to have that guy in his life with whom he could be goofy, with whom he could fix cars and learn to shave. I thought he needed me as a constant presence in his life, imperfect as I was. To Cindi, that was selfish, but to me, it was my way of showing that I cared.

The minute one parent is willing to jump through hoops to continue the relationship with the child, that's the minute the other parent wields the power. The parent who doesn't care whether the child sees the other parent calls all the shots. I was the only parent who cared about Charles seeing me. Therefore, Cindi called the shots.

We went through a time when she didn't want me to bring Charles to my folks' house because she hated my mom or my brothers. She thought they had sexually abused him. I worked very hard to continue their relationships, often sneaking him out there, because I knew he would need more than me in his corner later in life. I decided that if he could form bonds with my family, they could be my back-up. Cindi was always angry about his being at my folks' house and threatened to take my mom to court for, I guess, being a bad grandma. That never materialized, but my time in the legal process with Cindi was only beginning.

    I kept telling my lawyer to give her whatever she wanted. Then her lawyer would come back and ask for more. It was just a game to her lawyer. If you don't ask, you don't get it, I guess. There was no sense of conscience between the two of them, Cindi and her lawyer. It was just gimme, gimme, gimme. And I gave. You want money to repair your car? Sure. You want money for my having Charles in your daycare? Sure. You want money for the escrow to fix the boulevard in front of your house? Sure. You want me to pay off our credit cards? Sure. The list was endless. I just tried to keep throwing money at her, in and out of court. I didn't even have the money, but I figured I would find a way somehow.

    All of this was affecting me, though I would not have admitted it at the time. I was horribly depressed and ever-anxious, ever on edge. Whenever I went to pick up Charles, I knew what to expect: anger, screaming, and full-on resentment. Every time I approached the house, my breaths grew short, my heart raced, I would start to sweat, and I would feel like I was going to pass out. Pure hopelessness would set in. Cindi's presence would create a horrible hole in my stomach that I can only explain as a feeling of pure despair. You wouldn't think one person would be able to do that, but the fear of losing my son was maliciously real. Cindi often talked about taking him to Colorado and living with her mom if I didn't do what she asked. Her leaving with Charles would probably have been illegal, but how long would it have taken the courts to get her back to Minnesota? Here I was, trying to build bridges for Charles, and she was following behind, setting them on fire.

    My department head at work, Heidi, was very understanding. I told her I would do everything possible not to have all of this affect my work but that I was also in a tough spot. I warned her that Cindi might try to come to the school and make a scene. She was so unpredictable, I just didn't know what to expect and wanted Heidi to know what was going on should anything happen. She understood. She had been abused by her ex-husband for many years. Apparently, he had been similar to Cindi. It explained why Heidi always looked out for the little guys, the faculty, while taking the heat from the administration. Heidi and I ended up with a mutual admiration during all the trouble I was experiencing. She understood and was so proud of the job I was doing in spite of my personal problems. It was great to have that support. She became my work mom.

Our usual exchange, ever after, was like this: the administration would hear about some crazy teaching practices going on in Augustine's classroom. Then Heidi would come "spy" on me, like what she saw, and turn around and tell the administrators why the class was doing such-and-such, the purpose of my lesson plan, and its effectiveness with the students. This was long before I knew what a Rubric was and how to defend my own lesson plans.

Heidi went to bat for me more than once, and before long, she had the whole administration on my side. They would send new teachers to me to learn how to teach effectively and creatively, and they would send the "problem" students to me who hated their English classes because I could retain them. For a college, the retention of money (a.k.a. students) is the one and only impetus behind every decision. Somewhere far down the list is the students and how their future is being affected. Once in a while, when a college is losing money, that small subject is briefly brushed past. Then the college pulls out the retention banners from the closet and parades them in front of the teachers. The message couldn't be any plainer: make us more money now! But what they call that is retention. It is "for the students' sake."

Basic retention of students was never a problem for me because I knew what they were thinking: taking an English class if you are going into something like interior design seems a lot like highway robbery, especially when the class was self-admittedly a brush-up class. I know the equation from that statement to retention of students may seem to be missing some steps, but the equation has to first involve the people who are actually required to take the class. The most important aspect of communication is understanding one's audience. The rest of the equation falls in place from there. And the classroom is all about communication. I made sure mine was mostly positive communication, because regardless of how long the students had been out of high school, they remembered and expected negative communication in an

English class. You know: red marks all over the paper you slaved away on. I couldn't believe how many people had had traumatic experiences in high school English.

Most high schools have done a pretty good job of making people groan when the words "English" and "Class" are uttered in the same breath. How much time did we all spend in those classes? I understood what most students, the good and the not-so-good ones, were thinking and feeling: to get basically the same thing you got in high school right out of the shoot, it was a real "you gotta be kidding me" feeling for the them. Hadn't they suffered enough in high school?

But the beauty of teaching English was that I was able to get into some of the interesting stuff about the language and the creative process that apparently no one had ever gotten to in high school. My class was a bit of an eye-opener for many students, and I had a hell of a lot of fun. I was neither a grammar Nazi nor a fine-toothed editor, though I could be both when appropriate.

I was far more attuned to the creative process, that thing that gets stomped out of most people by teachers. The creative process is what writes proposals, and emails, and resumes, and copy for radio, and letters of intent and advertisements for your business…everything. Without the ability to utilize your creativity, you sit there staring at a blank paper or computer screen and become angry because you know you can't do it. How do you know you can't do it? Because of crappy experiences with crappy grading systems.

Unfortunately, what we rarely, if ever, were graded on in school was the first draft: the horrible version of the eventual product. The most important thing you will do when writing anything. Nobody seemed to tell us that. So much attention was given to what a paper looked like in the end that we began to believe that every word needed to come out "right," or we were just wasting our time. Then, when we couldn't get it to look "right" (whatever that means) immediately, we became frustrated, and *boom!* We thought that what we were doing was writing something terrible and we gave up. That's a lot of people's creative process.

So what I did was to say forget the finished product. That is secondary, if that, because if you have nothing to work with in the first place, you will end up with nothing. Your first ideas, dumb as they may be, are the most important part of creating anything. Jot them down, all of them. Map them, list them, web them, write them. Use whatever technique from whatever textbook you want. It is all the same idea: get the good and the bad stuff on the page. Once a student got as much as he or she could onto the paper, we could make the rest happen in class together. But we needed something to work with in the first place.

I would say, "Write it on a napkin or a cereal box and turn that in." For some reason, students loved that idea: the first draft could look like crap and still be worth something in my class. I really didn't care what the draft looked like at first read, as long as it was something. The first draft, in any condition, was half the paper's grade. That's pretty good encouragement when you've already got 50/100 just for writing something...anything.

I actually was encouraging crap. That was often a new concept for many students. No wonder the so-called problem students stayed in the class! Anyone can turn in crap. In fact, with most of my students, they felt that their specialty was, in fact, crap. In my class, we could work with crap. After all, we've all got to start somewhere. Starting with something awful meant only that we were starting, and that was at least half the battle. I was amazed by how many people hadn't been told that concept prior to my class. It was like a life jacket for someone who was drowning in a perception of his or her own terrible writing ability. Getting half the paper's grade for something awful was good news for someone used to barely getting Ds in writing. Heck, it was good news for someone who was used to getting As.

Then, of course, the bad news would come, but in a slightly new light. Quite simply, each paper would have a version of this written on it: here's how many more points you would get if you called this your final draft, and here's what to do to get more points – or – here is where the draft you just turned in falls on the continuum between the 50 points you have now and the 100 points that will get you an A+. The rough and final draft could score a total of 60/100 if turned in again as it was originally written, and someone could walk away with a D on the paper.

That was a pretty normal occurrence, a rough draft equaling 10/50 points were it turned in as a final draft. Once in a while someone would take me up on the 60/100 on their paper, but usually students would look at my comments and say, "This is all I need to do to get an A?" Once you have something to work with, the editing really is all that's left. Sometimes the editing is hard, and sometimes it is easy, but if you do it in steps, a little at a time, it really isn't the perplexity that we were led to believe it is. It's just like any other process. You just do it until you are satisfied and until you think your audience is going to understand it.

Everything needed to be modeled several ways, several times, and I did that for them, writing along with them during my own exercises. They needed to see it many ways and many times, and they needed to see it from me as well as their peers. Once students saw and began to try the creative and the editing processes, the whole thing turned into small steps that were tolerable.

Meanwhile, the same kind of process was happening with Kim and me. My head was crammed full of all the crap from my marriage. What Kim was telling me without saying it was she could work with my crap. Our relationship was a mirror image of my classroom. And I was learning she would give me opportunity after opportunity to get better.

In my class, there were no limits on drafts. If a student turned in draft #2 and was satisfied with 70/100, so be it. If another student turned in draft #8 and still wasn't satisfied with 98/100, a draft #9 was fine with me. Complete control of your own destiny with lots of help or no help if you didn't want it; everything was up to the student. I set the standard, and they could take it or leave it knowing they had the control. *That* is communication. That's how you keep people interested and learning even though they initially didn't want to be there. The quality was not compromised and neither was the students' integrity. Besides putting the students' grades in their own hands, I also made sure to keep the class fun and different from a high school experience.

If you are having fun, the learning will not only follow, but it won't seem so painful. My classroom was a bit of a slapstick comedy act, a bit of truthfulness in defiance of the norms I was supposed to uphold, a bit of hand-holding, a bit of storytelling followed by a relevant exercise, and a lot of listening on my part. I also made sure to get to things that my students had never thought of but which were relevant to them as participants in the English language.

For example, the first thing we covered was the European tribes at the end of the Roman Empire and how their pidgin language, which was used only to do business, turned into the language we now speak. Of course, starting classes with the origins of English brought forth responses like, "Why are you telling us this?" But if you can imagine that this language we use every day began as a handful of words that many tribes had in common for trading, and that families soon found themselves using the common words at home, and that eventually a guy named Geoffrey Chaucer began writing stories using the shared trading language…suddenly you realize what a melting pot of words, borrowed from everywhere, English has always been. It was a bit like, "This is our language" to its first speakers – not the church's and not the governments'. It belonged to its speakers.

It's a provocative thought. It really makes the way you think of your language seem a little less scholarly and a little more real. English is ever-changing and is still based on choices its speakers make, not on choices handed down by lame-ass English teachers as it so often feels like in school. I loved turning people on to that idea. The hairs on the back of my neck would stand up as I watched students become excited and interested in hearing things they'd never heard before. We would follow a fictional tribe through trading and take-overs, each step along the way adding just a little extra flavor to the growing creole or hybrid that English was becoming – little bits of different languages all mixed together.

I would add to the mix the discovery and colonization of North America and all the new flavors from that melting pot creole, eventually showing how English simmered into today's language. For example, we got words like "Geronimo" which went from the Native American warrior to paratroopers in WWI, and finally to Looney Toons cartoons. Now we all know what to yell when jumping off a cliff. Or a word like Kamikaze which went from Japanese pilots in WWII to a drink for someone who is daring and who possibly has a death wish. Or the word jazz, which now means easy listening, but in the late 1800s in the brothels of New Orleans meant roughly the same as fuck. So if you went to get "jassed," you went to fuck. And the band that was playing while you were doing it became known as a "jass" or jazz band, quite literally a fuck band. No scholar would ever have deemed that word acceptable for common linguistic use. But there it is.

Add the advent of the Internet and modern things we say which would have been completely foreign a few years ago such as Googling something or streaming music, and students began to see that English still belongs to us all. I could watch reactions and see students start to like the idea that the choices they made shaped their own language. The classic questions of whether 'ain't' is a word ended up being utterly silly. Suddenly, whether or not your audience can understand what you write became the focus.

Students found themselves in charge of what they wrote, and they ate up that notion. Provided you keep your audience in mind, you can do whatever you want – it was a completely new concept to a lot of people. English is actually a living, breathing entity, always being reinvented and revitalized by those who breathe life into it: us. That was a cool thought to a lot of students.

The same came to be true of relationships to me. The living, breathing entity which was my relationship with Kim could be sustained warmly and equally, rather than coldly and singularly by one who dictates and one who is subservient. But it takes two. In the classroom and in my personal life, I was closely learning which type of relationship I preferred.

To me, except for Cindi's ominous presence, the classroom represented a hell of a good time most every day and was incredibly healing and helpful to my learning about relationships. The students could feel it too, I think. They got a lot of laughs, real help in their writing processes, and even a little real-life perspective. I loved it. My classes ended up being viewed as a pretty good requirement even though students groaned when they first saw 'English' on their schedules. I just tried to show them a good time while actually showing them things they could use. My buddy, a math professor, called me an edu-tainer. And I loved edu-taining.

Still, it was becoming tougher to keep my positive attitude and creativity in the midst of the daily onslaughts from Cindi. I would have a good class, then get a phone call from Cindi, and I was right back to where I had started: hell. By time I left the building at night, I was usually exhausted from trying to keep my head up. Still, roller-coasters as most days were, I would eventually end up back at Kim's and be recharged, rehealed, and reloved. Unfortunately, it was becoming more and more of a chore for Kim to pull me back from the edge. My disgusting sewage was beginning to seep into paradise.

I came home one night to Kim's apartment with a horrible pain in my head. I remember it being an especially troublesome day with Cindi, and I also had to jump in and teach a class for someone who had called in sick. I had done a lot of literal and figurative thinking on my feet. I guess it seemed a bit like playing goalie, trying to defend all of Cindi's shots and also defending our program to a few disgruntled students.

When I got home, I was beginning to realize I had a sinus infection and a horrible migraine. I felt like I was going to throw up, and my head was killing me. I walked in, said nothing to Kim, went straight to the bathroom, and sat on my knees by the toilet. She followed me and spoke through the almost-closed door.

"Are you ok?"

"No." I quietly moaned.

"Can I come in?"

"Yes."

"What's wrong?"

"Ah! Turn off the light," I said from the floor, shielding my eyes.

"Sorry. What can I do?" The light clicked off.

The pain was awful, perhaps more so now that I was able to let down my guard and not perform for the outside world. "I don't know. I think I have a sinus infection. I get them sometimes," I said painfully. "Maybe a migraine, too. I feel like I'm gonna puke."

"What do you need, baby?"

"Antibiotics. But I don't want to go to the doctor."

"I wish I had some left over. I used to have some."

"Do you know where The Wedge is?"

"Uptown?"

"Franklin and Lyndale. I need some Goldenseal tincture in Sage tea. And some Advil for migraines. That might work."

"Ok, I'll be right back."

"I'm so sorry, honey."

"No problem."

"Can you turn on the shower? Maybe steam would help until you get back."

"Yes!"

The shower went on, and then she was gone. I had walked in and more or less made her go out into the cold on a crazy mission. I felt awful for her and disappointed in myself. I sat in the corner on the bathroom floor, in agony, and wished for something else: another life, another fate, anything. All I had was Kim, but I knew I couldn't keep doing this to her – couldn't keep taking advantage of her with my problems. She deserved better. She deserved a guy who wasn't from the hellish sewer that I was. She deserved so much more. I was a joke. I wasn't a whole person. She was in love with a shell of a guy. She thought I was something I was not.

Cindi knew. She knew the real me: a disastrous, pathetic, asshole loser with whom she had made the biggest mistake of her life. Whatever she had seen in me, whatever Kim was now seeing, was about to erode. Cindi knew what was underneath and soon Kim would too. It was a horrifying thought that throbbed in my head on Kim's bathroom floor. I was still there when she got back. She made the tea, gave me some migraine pills, and fed me a few other things someone at the coop suggested I try. I tried it all right there on the floor. She sat next to me and rubbed my back. Her only desire was that I feel better. She was so wonderful.

When I began to feel better, either from all the crazy organic cures or from the placebo effect, I decided I had to tell her what I had been thinking.

"Kim, honey, I can't keep doing this to you. I'm a horrible guy to go out with, much less to be your boyfriend."

"What? No, you're not."

"Look at what I did tonight. I'm a horrible mess. This is not what you need."

"You can't tell me what I need. I need you."

"I know you think you do, but I have to at least make one good decision for the both of us. If I stay here, you will get too attached to me. I think I have to set you free."

"I'm not a dog, John. You can't decide that for me."

"I have to. There's a lot you don't know. There's a lot you should not have to deal with."

"John, I *want* to deal with your shit. I want to help you. I love you!"

"You don't love me, Kim. You don't know me."

"I *do* know you, and I know what an awesome guy you are. I love you, damn it!"

"You think that now, but it's not true, and you won't always think that. I'm not who you think."

"Are you breaking up with me? After I went and got you the stuff that made you feel better? I helped you feel better so you could break up with me? I can't believe you!"

"See, Kim, this is what I am talking about. I'm actually a horrible person."

"Why?" The tears were beginning to form.

"That's just the way I am. Cindi knows it."

"*Cindi is an idiot!*" Down they came.

"But she knows me, and she's right about me. Deep down, I'm ugly. I'm awful."

"She is lying to you to manipulate you. Don't you see that?" She wiped the tears away from her face.

"No, she's right. I'm a different person around her. That's the real me. Not this guy. You're seeing the good version of me."

"Because you *are* good!" She sniffed.

"No, I'm not, Kim. I wish I were, but I'm not."

"You are with me for a reason! I will show you that the good version of you *is* you!"

"I'm with you because I thought I needed your help. I made a bad decision by dragging you into this. That's all I do. I make bad decision after bad decision. And I have to stop it. I have to stop here before I really hurt you. I am using you, Kim."

"That makes no sense, John! If you don't love me then go. You don't have to make up a bunch of crap!"

"I do love you, Kim. You're the most wonderful girl I have ever met! That's why I am saying this. I have to hurt you now before it gets worse, because you don't deserve to have this be your life. You deserve a better life. You deserve a better guy!"

"I *do* deserve a better guy, and he's you, you jackass!"

"Kim, I'm sorry, but I have made up my mind. I have to do the right thing."

"What right thing? John, listen to yourself! You love me, so the right thing is to dump me?"

"Yes."

"Cindi is making you do this?"

"No. Kim, between my making your life miserable, and..."

"You are not making my life miserable!"

"Enough nights like tonight, and you will be miserable. I know it."

"You are being ridiculous. I was completely happy to go get your things to make you feel better. I am not miserable, I am happy! I can help you because I *love you*, John! Please understand that!"

"I *do* understand it. I don't know what else to do, Kim. I am going to drag you down with me, and I don't want that to happen to you. I love you. I want you to have a great life. This ain't it."

I paused a moment. It was sinking in, I thought.

"Kim, I don't want you to come to our last show. I just can't have you go through all this."

"That's crazy. Of course I am going to come."

"No. You are not to come under any circumstance."

"John, that is enough!" she said emphatically. "I will make the decisions tonight. You are not in a place to decide anything. I am your girlfriend, and you need to stop and listen to me. Do you understand me?"

"Yes."

"Ok. We are not talking about this now. You will get into bed, and we will talk about this tomorrow when you are rested."

"Ok."

"Come on, you grumpy-ass." She grabbed my arm and pulled it, so I got up. "Into bed with you. You're tired, and it's past your bedtime. Come on."

Dutifully, without hesitation, I followed. She took off my clothes and moved the blankets back for me. When I lay down, she covered me up.

"I am going to get my book, and I will be right back. Stay here."

I closed my eyes. I don't remember her coming back. I only remember waking up and seeing her sweet face there the next morning. It was so good to be in that bed with her. Somehow she knew how to wash away all the shit from my day and put paradise back to its original splendor.

From the Abyss   John Emil Augustine

One More Time

Date: Fri Nov 30, 2001, 10:27 am
Subject: Our last show this Saturday

Hey, it's our last show this Saturday, December 1st at 9:30 pm. Uptown Bar on Hennepin and Lake in Uptown Minneapolis. Hope we'll see you one last time tomorrow night!

Hope to see ya there!

As hard as Kim worked to fix my broken spirit, I was constantly torn. What was I going to do? She was so good for me, but that was a selfish way to look at our relationship. I was not good for her. I was toxic. Was I helping her? Did she need to mother me? Was this relationship possibly good for her despite my reservations? It was so confusing. I was trying to do the right thing, but what was right? Every time I thought I had it figured out, the right thing eluded me.

I walked into Kim's apartment the Saturday before the show. Her cousin, Trish, was there. Trish was also a knockout blonde. It was kind of amazing how different they looked but how equally hot they were. They were both in sweatpants, and I felt out of place in my show clothes: black tweed slacks and jacket with my bright green silk shirt, green kufi, and black boots. Her cousin was eager to talk to me.

"Hi, I'm Trish, Kim's cousin from Iowa." She pulled her hair back with a scrunchie to hide its messiness in her unprepared state.

"Great. I'm John." I offered my hand.

"I hear you have a show tonight." Trish squeezed my hand while her other hand fumbled with the scrunchie.

"Yeah, last one."

"Their band is really good," Kim said.

"Why is this your last show?"

"Everyone's going their separate ways. We may end up recruiting some new guys and playing out again, but we don't really know. We just want to make the last one kick ass tonight."

"Can we come?" Trish asked.

Kim glanced at me. She remembered what I had said and was wondering if I was actually serious about it. But I couldn't let her down, not in front of her cousin. "Yeah. I'll put you both on the guest list. Just say you are with us and tell them your names."

Kim brightened up. "We'll be on the guest list! How cool!"

Outside, it was snowing. Big flakes floated gracefully in the air, down to the ground to accumulate just slightly on the brown grass. There wouldn't be much snow that year. Like everything I was experiencing, the temperatures would roller-coaster up and down to places no one in Minnesota would have expected: high highs and low lows. I sat down on the secondhand couch, a bizarre contrast to its plainness in my show clothes, and watched the large, lofty flakes dance.

"You're an English professor?" I turned back to the girls who were still standing.

"Almost. I'm studying for my assistant professorship. So I'm not officially a professor yet."

"But you teach college English?"

"Yep."

"He's such a good teacher, too. I know some of his students. They love him!" Kim added.

"I had better watch what I say around you. We don't know anyone who is an English professor," Trish said admiringly.

Again, there I was, the magical figure in Kim's life. She was gloating over me, and Trish was admiring. Could I do nothing to un-impress them? "You can talk any which way you want, Trish. I only pay attention when I'm reading papers."

"That's so cool. You're totally not stuck up!"

"I told you, Trish." Kim smiled.

"No, not stuck up." I said blankly.

"Do you have a brother?" she wanted to know.

"That's funny. Yeah, two of them, but they are much younger. The oldest is 14."

"I guess I can wait a few years."

"Trish!" Kim scolded.

"Sorry!" She laughed. "I'm just so happy for Kim. You're a keeper!"

Jesus, they almost had me convinced about how great I was! I suppose when your whole family is from a blue collar background in a small Iowa town, an English teacher who is a musician in Minneapolis is about the greatest person these young girls could think to have as a boyfriend. In my family, I was on the lowest rung in terms of schooling and occupation. And no one in my family liked that I was a musician. It was the equivalent of a bum. Add to that my baby and failed marriage – I wasn't exactly admired. My whole family just felt bad for how I had ended up. It's like when a plane crashes, and everyone thinks, "Well, that's that. Better gather the body parts and plane pieces."

But to Kim's family, I was almost a celebrity. How strange it is, the way you look at a thing. The same exact guy, I could be horrible and wonderful simultaneously. It just depended on the looker and the position from which I was viewed. Perhaps I was an asshole and a dead-beat dad. Cindi may have been right from her perspective. At the same time, maybe I was a good dad. Kim may have been correct from the way she saw things. Would Kim change her mind about me? What had first appeared so great with Cindi had quickly turned bad. Would Kim, perhaps like Emily, constantly be like this? Could she remain strong, fun, devoted, and wonderful, the way she was now? Or did it have to do with me and the way she saw me? When she really did know me and all the horrible stuff about me, would she be so determined to help me? Or would her determination keep me the way I was when I was around her? Was I a good guy because of her?

"Well, I've got my problems. I may not be as much a keeper as I first appear."

"I know you're in the middle of a divorce. Just you and Kim let me know what you need me to do to help."

Her cousin wanted to help me? What was with this family? They accepted my divorce? "It's pretty nasty. I feel like I shouldn't even be dragging Kim into this." I glanced at her.

Quickly she said, "But it's too late! I already love you!"

"You stick with Kim. You'll get through this. Kim needs a good, educated man. Someone who will be good to her. She adores you and will always help."

"Well, I'll try. It's not easy at the moment, I'm afraid."

"It doesn't matter. I like you. I have a good feeling about you. Kim, your mom will love him."

"Think so?" she asked.

"I know so."

I couldn't help but feel I was getting quickly dragged in over my head. But her family was turning out to be so darn nice that it didn't seem to matter.

Kim and Trish felt like the biggest VIPs that night. A guest of our band. The girlfriend of the keyboard player. The cousin of the girlfriend. For them, being in the city and having an in with the city's then-hot band must have been pretty cool. We were charming onstage. When it's your last show, people hang on your every word, knowing they will never see the spectacle again. I remember getting a lot of laughs between songs, followed by shouts for us not to split up. I'm sure it was really quite a show for Trish and Kim to witness. Every time I looked over, they were pointing and looking at me.

"We hope you'll all be around for the new incarnation of our band. We're all gonna get back together right here at the Uptown and rock again very soon!" I promised the crowd. The room exploded with shouts and cheers. Then we broke into our encore, and the room went nuts. People smashed their glasses and danced like they were crazy. One last time to rock with the band.

Then it was over. But it was the start of a great month. Maybe my last great month for many, many years.

A New Year

December '01 was an incredible month even though there was nothing specifically incredible about it. Everything went on as usual, but there was something different. I had finally let myself go and just went with Kim. I remember that after the show I went back home with her. Trish slept on the couch while Kim and I retired to her bedroom. When we woke up the next morning, Trish left. Then Kim made me follow her into the shower. Standing there, under the warm water, looking at Kim naked and beautiful in front of me was more a paradise than I ever had ever imagined. She just cuddled up tight against me, and we stood there kissing under the water. It was heaven.

I remember small things. We watched the Reece Witherspoon movie in which she goes to college to get a law degree. I remember thinking how much Kim was like Reece's character: smart and cute. So determined and full of spunk. A lot like Emily, too. I remember every morning when I left her apartment, Kim would come out of the bedroom wrapped in nothing but her comforter, quickly pack me a lunch, kiss me goodbye, and tell me to have a good day.

Complete support. It was so foreign to me. She never tried to maliciously attack me or harbor unknown grudges against me. She never told me I was a loser or a bad person. Everything she did was the opposite of that. Everything she did was the opposite of every bad relationship I had been in. She was a genuinely good person and a wonderful-beyond-words girlfriend. Like a dry sponge, at first I would deflect her and whatever magical substance she possessed which rehydrated my soul. But soon I was soaking it in and reawakening – actually, awakening – to our life. Awakening to a good relationship.

Kim did things to me that no one had ever done: spiritually, sexually, and intellectually. She was all the things I wasn't and everything I wished for in a girl. I admired every single inch. She was not perfect, but I began to realize that someone can be imperfect and still perfect at the same time. The imperfections by airbrush standards suddenly seemed so stupid. Who wanted that? The reality was so much richer and better. The word perfect became immaterial. Imperfect was far better.

I remember pulling up to her apartment building most nights with my noisy truck. Her window faced the street, and she knew the sound of my vehicle. By the time I had parallel parked, Kim would usually be in the apartment building doorway so I wouldn't have to ring her. She was always so excited to see me. I was excited to see her, too.

Sometimes she would have straightened her hair, so it was soft and shiny-blonde against her shoulders. Sometimes she would leave it curly, and sweet little spirals hung down around her face. It was kind of like going out with two different girls, except both were singularly wonderful, singularly Kim. If I didn't see her in the doorway of the apartment, hanging her beautiful hair out into the cold, I would get a few things together in my bag to buy a minute of time. Then I would look up, and there she would be, beaming her warm sunshiny smile at me. I would walk toward her, engulfed in her love.

New Year's Eve brought back Trish and a few other cousins and friends. I was in an apartment full of beautiful girls. It was so crazy. And they all loved me. There really was a first time for everything! We went to The Library Bar in Dinkytown for the night. I would have rather been playing because I always thought it was the greatest honor for a musician to be asked to play on New Year's Eve, but I was beginning to see why my buddies with girlfriends had wanted the night off.

All night, Kim's friends and cousins asked me about myself, and though it seems selfish, it felt so cool that they adored me. I was blown away by it. None adored me more than Kim. I sat beside her all night and admired her every word, her every move. It was probably the best New Year's Eve I had ever experienced, and I wasn't even playing the gig. Then there was the New Year's Eve kiss which Kim made sure happened and even planned an hour ahead of time. She kissed me and said, "This is the beginning of the first good year you will spend with me. Everything else in our lives has led up to this year. I will make you as happy as you have made me. I love you so much, baby."

I said, "I love you too." We both had tears in our eyes until one of the girls threw confetti at us and happily broke the moment. I don't think I had ever felt more hopeful, more loved, and more like it didn't matter what move I made or thing I said. As long as I had Kim, I could not go wrong. Her healing salve, words mixed lovingly with close contact and laughter, were all I needed. It had all soaked in, and I knew I never wanted to be without her. I was surprised to be so happy and also so un-self-conscious about it. I was beyond happy, and for the first time in a long time, I didn't feel guilty about feeling that way. Anything that went wrong, Kim and I would meet head-on as a team. No problem would be too great for us.

The next morning, not being able to sleep, I was up by 7 and out the door by 7:05. I went to my favorite bakery, A Baker's Wife on Cedar Avenue in South Minneapolis, and luckily, they happened to be open. I bought an assortment of rolls and donuts. Then I went to the grocery store and picked up some fresh ingredients to mix with scrambled eggs: chives, tomatoes, ham, mushrooms, garlic, chalets, and some cilantro. I also picked up some tomato juice, orange juice, pickles, olives, and salt and pepper for mimosa, screwdrivers, and Bloody Marys. Everything else, including English muffins, jam, butter, and coffee, we had at home.

By 9:00, I was back, and everyone else was still sound asleep. I began to cook. Before long, the smell of coffee, toasted English muffins, and eggs with all the chopped ingredients began to rouse all the sleepy heads. Hung over and groggy, the girls in their baggy flannel jammies, oversized shirts, messed up hair, and smeared make-up came to the kitchen and happily took whatever looked good to them. There was something for everyone, and everyone perked up pretty quickly. I suppose it was a point-scoring moment for me, but I just wanted all Kim's statements about her boyfriend to be true, so her family and friends could see firsthand that she had made a good choice.

Trish was the last one to wake up. She had had a rough night. She came out and hugged me and thanked me. Everyone wanted to know why, and she told how I had held her hair the night before while she puked in Kim's bathroom. That sealed the deal. They all expected me the next month in Iowa for their next get-together. I was officially one of the family.

To be part of such a nice family was like nothing I had ever felt. Being accepted into Cindi's family had been weird. They all tried to act how they thought a normal family should act. It was a little creepy and altogether awkward. Later, I found out what they were like and how much they disliked each other. Only my father-in-law turned out to be cool. He would be the only one I would really miss. And he was just a third husband.

Despite my warm feeling on that cold winter day, I knew reality was waiting just outside Kim's apartment. Although happy and cozy inside with all the girls, I knew that the snow-flecked air outside, so sparkly and white, was far different than one might expect. Outside, where the puffy pink slippers and thin jammies would have been of little comfort, the frigid air hung all around us, ominous and harsh. I had just been out there. I knew. No one else was thinking about it, but I knew it was there, waiting. It's funny how something so beautiful, once experienced completely and up-close, can be so uncomfortable and unforgiving.

I would protect Kim from it. I knew I could. I could be that guy. I could be a good boyfriend.

A Weird Turn

Saying goodbye later that day to the girls as they prepared to drive home, I really thought I would see them in Iowa the next month. I had been accepted. It felt great. I was about to be *the* boyfriend. They had always wanted someone who would be better, cooler, smarter, and worldlier than Kim's high school boyfriend in Iowa. They all knew Kim would go to Minneapolis and find the perfect guy for herself. That visit had proven they were right. However, the guy they met, the one who was perfect for Kim, was already in way over his head elsewhere. It didn't appear so at the time, but the danger was all around. All it took was for me to walk out of that warm apartment into the cold January morning. Oh, that I could have stayed, hidden, wrapped in Kim, and lived, warm and loved, in her arms.

But there were lawyers about. The vast court system had my number, and my time was up. Shivering and afraid in Downtown St. Paul, I walked to the courthouse and dropped my wallet and keys into the unfriendly gray tubs that went, day in and day out, through the X-ray machine. Security didn't care who I was, how I was, or what my intentions were. They were only scanning my possessions as they scanned everybody's who came through the court mill. Set 'em up and knock 'em down. The security team, the lawyers, and certainly the judge could have cared less who I was, who Cindi was, and what our problems were. They only cared that they pushed us through one side and out the other. Every day, the same. In and out, next, in and out, next.

The marble floor and pillars; the audacious, hard shininess was ominous. So much money had been put into the effect of the towering, enigmatic tallness of the entryway. It felt as though the building itself looked down on me as if I were nothing. The court system was an expensive-looking used car lot which evoked my every anxiety. Could I bargain, or couldn't I? In how many sentences could my lawyer be effective? Time was money: my money. The system was just an over-priced game that was way out of my league.

The good news that came in the little courtroom on the second floor, one of the many with beautiful, expensive woodwork and blandly painted walls, was that it was not legal for Cindi to be on my insurance for more than a few months after the divorce was settled. That was too bad, because she planned to go into business for herself with the daycare and would have extremely expensive insurance because of being self-employed. Or none at all. She also was not allowed alimony as we hadn't been married long enough for her to establish that she was no longer relevant in the workforce. Alimony is for spouses who have lived off the "family" income for a certain amount of years, I was told. We simply hadn't been married long enough.

The judge was hesitant to let me pay off all the credit cards, so he split them up. He also did not want me to give my half of the house away scot-free, but I convinced him to let me do it as I glanced at the angry stare across from me.

Cindi was fuming, and we all could see it. She had been convinced she would cash in much more than what the judge was decreeing. I didn't feel good or bad about it. I just thought, "Hey, if this is the law, what are we going to do? I tried, anyway." I knew Cindi would ask for money outside of court, but Kim and I could talk it over and decide what we felt was right. I wasn't alone in all this, despite being surrounded by the empty enormity of the court process.

Afterward, Cindi left the building as quickly as she could, and I figured I would get the phone call to top all phone calls the next day. But it never came. It was such a relief mixed with a whisper of a threat. Would the call eventually come, perhaps inflated with each day it waited? By that time, I knew enough to know I could expect the unexpected from Cindi. Still, I tried to think of what turn to expect, though it did me no good. She was impossible to predict.

After a few days, I forgot about the courtroom and settled back into the warmth of Kim's apartment. But every morning, I went out into the cold to my truck. Every day, the threat of Cindi's phone call hung over me. That beautiful, sparkly silence outside the window was a cold, suffocating scream waiting to happen. I would be unprepared, unaware of what to do when it caught me off guard, unprotected.

I was at my parents' house. My cell phone rang. I answered without even thinking.

And there was Cindi's voice.

I inhaled quickly, surprised. This was the call. My folks were about to hear the phone call from hell. I quickly rushed downstairs into an empty room and shut the door. It would be long. It would be loud. I would not know what to say. She would eventually be right, because she was making the fuss. My day was about to nose-dive.

"I was wondering..." she started.

"Here it comes," I thought. "She's going to get me to say something and then: bam!"

"Hello?" she said.

I could pretend to not hear her. I could hang up. I could...take it like a man, I guessed. "Yeah?"

"I said I was wondering..."

"Ok."

"You sound sick or really quiet or something. Are you ok? Did you lose your voice?"

"She's really baiting me," I thought. What kind of a messed up call was this turning out to be?

"John?"

"Huh? Yeah? I'm ok."

"Ok. You sound weird."

"Oh, sorry." She already had me apologizing. This was not going well.

"You're ok?"

Oh my God, what was she trying to do? "I'm fine."

"Can you talk?"

"Yeah."

"I was wondering...Charles keeps saying 'Dadda' when we are eating at the table. I think he wants you to be here. Would you come over and eat with him?"

"What?"

"Well, I'm not sure, but I want to see if that's what he is asking. I'm just trying to see if he is really asking for you to eat with him."

"Ok."

"What are you doing tonight?"

"Nothing."

"Ok. Would you be comfortable coming over here and eating dinner with Charles?"

"Sure."

"Nothing fancy. We're just having Mac and Cheese and maybe some hot dogs or something. Kid food."

"Ok."

"5:00?"

"Sure."

"Ok. See you then."

"Bye."

"Bye."

That was the weird unexpectedness for which I could never prepare.

Don't Look Back

It wasn't that Cindi was nice that night, although she was. It wasn't that being there in my old house was all that great. Frankly, it was unnerving. It wasn't that she was happy to see Charles and I having fun, though she was. It wasn't that she wanted me to put him to bed and stay and talk afterward. It wasn't that she was wearing perfume and a cute shirt that was tight and made her boobs look good. It wasn't that I was still attracted to her. It was that she asked me if there was any way we could repair what we had done. It was, even if only a small possibility had emerged, that Charles could have a dad and a mom both, together. Wearing my old lock and chain didn't matter. Only Charles mattered.

The daycare toys were in bins around the dining room in the dark. The candle on the living room TV was dripping wax. The moonlight shone through the back door. And I kissed her. After all of that, with just one visit I allowed myself back into the abyss. It felt neither good nor bad. It was, in fact, neither. It was what I, as a married man, must do. I knew I must.

Son, I married her for better or for worse. For better or for worse.

If Charles had a second shot at learning what a marriage was about, I needed to do whatever I could to give him that. He needed to see a marriage that worked. I could be a good husband.

But wait. What about being a good boyfriend? How could I accomplish both? I couldn't. I couldn't do both. What now?

So I left. Roared away in my truck to think. I pulled into an empty lot and turned the engine off in the moonlight. This was not what I had expected. This was the worst two choices I could have imagined. But there was Charles.

There was Charles.

I couldn't think of me. I couldn't think of Cindi. I couldn't...I dared not think it...I couldn't. I couldn't think of...but I had to. There was Charles. But I had to be a good boyfriend. But what if Charles could grow up in a two-parent home? He needed to see that. He needed, for his future family, to develop those skills. I needed to model them. I had to show him how to be a good dad. Kim…sweet, beautiful Kim…what would she do? Kim.

My heart ached. She was everything. She was the one. She could do no wrong in my eyes. Everything about her was love. I had never been immersed so well in love. That was Kim: she was love. But what was I to Charles? Was I love? I was the recipient of great waves of anger. I was the recipient of hate. I was a lightning rod. Still, were I to make amends, make myself available to be a dad, I could be to Charles what Kim had been to me: love. But poor Kim. What would I do? I couldn't have this both ways.

I must have sat there for hours. It would not be fair to cheat on Kim with my wife. How crazy that sounds! I had to be, either way, completely dedicated. Oh, how, I wondered, did I end up in this situation? Why was I supposed to choose? Someone would inevitably get hurt. It seemed to me that it would be either Charles or Kim. A parent can't consider his own feelings or wants. The minute you have that baby in your arms, you give up some choices. You give up 'me first.' You take on 'child first' and don't look back. You can't look back. The child is there and is completely in need of your help.

But if you are, as I was, so distraught that you can't even help yourself, much less a child, who does that help? If the lifeguard jumps in with the shark attack victim, then there are two dead, not one. Unless the lifeguard can be successful. Then it's a different story. The lifeguard who out-maneuvers the shark turns the casualty into a second chance. Out-maneuvering a shark? Was the situation that dire? Was I considering trying to do the impossible? Did I really think I had a chance, after all we had been through, Cindi and I? What skills had I learned that winter to make me any better at dealing with the inevitable? *What should I do?*

I walked into Kim's apartment at ten that night. She had been crying. Her parents were having trouble. Her mom had left her dad that night. She needed me to hold her, and I did for a few minutes as we lay on her bed. Suddenly, I realized this was not going well. I couldn't commit to two girls. I sat up in bed.

"Kim, I have to tell you something."

"What? No, not now, honey. Please. I just need you here beside me."

"I can't, hon."

"Please. I need you right now. Please, John."

"Kim, this is going to hurt you, but I have to say it."

"What? No. Don't hurt me. Please." She sat up and looked at me. I had never seen her so scared.

It didn't matter. I had to tell her.

"Kim, I love you more than I have ever loved anyone in my life. I love you more than I can possibly say. You are…I can't say a word that means what you are to me. I love you so much."

"John! Shame on you! You scared me!"

"I have to tell you how I feel about you because I have to go."

"What? What are you…you're playing with me right now? John, come on! I'm not in the mood for this. Please, just hold me."

"Kim, I love you, but I have to go."

"Fine, where are you going that you can't lay here with me and hold me for a while? I am serious. I am so sad right now, and you are being cryptic. Stop it."

"I have to go."

"Fine, go! Then come back and hold me."

"I'm not coming back, Kim."

"What?"

"I am not coming back. Ever."

"John! What?" The tears formed quickly.

"I love you, Kim, but I have to go."

"John!" she shouted, drowning in her quickly mounting fear. "No!"

"Kim, I had to tell you."

"You said you love me!" Her voice quavered. "What are you doing? John, please stop." The tears rolled down her face.

"I'm sorry. I can't explain it. But I have to go." The words kept coming out, quietly and coldly. I could say nothing more and in no other way.

"You are breaking up with me? Now? John, I don't understand! Please don't! What can I do? What do you want from me?"

"Honey, I don't want anything. You are perfect the way you are, and I love everything about you."

"Then stay. John, please. Don't talk like this. Please, stay here. Please help me understand what you are doing."

I stood up. "I have to go."

"*John!*" she screamed.

"I love you, Kim."

She grabbed my arm, "John! You have to stay here! John! *John!*"

She was sobbing. I walked into the bathroom and grabbed a few things. She followed me.

"John, you don't…have to…do…this," she said between sobs.

"I am sorry, Kim," I said, completely deadpan. I felt nothing. I had to turn that part of me off. I could not feel anymore. I had to give that up.

I walked into the living room and grabbed a few video tapes from beneath the TV. "John! Stop it right now! Do not leave this room! I am your girlfriend! Listen to me! I can help you! *John!*"

Her screams were deafening. The crying horrendous. I was numb, focused on finding my possessions. The moment became a blur.

She grabbed hold of my shirt as hard as she could and ordered, "You stop this right now, John! I am your girlfriend. I am telling you to stop. Listen to me!"

"I have to go," I said, pulling away and opening the door.

"*JOOOOHNNNNNN!*" she screamed down the hall. The neighbors must have thought I was killing her. The door swung shut behind me forming a barrier between us.

The carpet was matted and frayed; junky, really. The walls were ugly, as ugly as they had been the first night I walked into this hallway. Yet the halogen lights were bright as if to highlight all its faults. As if to highlight mine. The sad cry behind the door ever so slowly faded as I walked toward the front of the building. It would be my last walk down that hall. It would be the first time I would walk down that hall and not feel excited to be there.

I did not look back.

Heart Hardened

I received an email from Kim a few days later. I remember a phrase from my early Bible studies in school: "But his heart was hardened." I'm not sure what story that is from, but I think possibly when Moses was trying to convince Pharaoh to let his people go, and the writer said Pharaoh's heart was hardened, and that's why he ignored Moses's pleas. That phrase went through my head more than once while reading Kim's subsequent emails.

Kim said she would give me time to think. She wanted me to come to my senses. She loved me. I told her I had to give my marriage a second try for Charles's sake. She said she felt that she had rightfully found and helped me. She was the winner, not Cindi. Cindi had forsaken me. Kim was who I truly belonged to. I must come to my senses.

But my heart was hardened.

Cindi and I spent some time just dating. We had good moments. We were trying to come back together. It was tricky. We slowly worked through things that were haunting us. Other things went unsaid. I had my moments during which I liked her and was even turned on, particularly by the idea that we could get back to being a family. I also had moments in which I was repulsed. She was still the same, and I could see that.

When I wasn't out with Cindi, I would call Elizabeth and ask to come over to her house for the evening; we would have wine and watch a movie. It was a respite. It wasn't Kim's, but that was for the better. Liz understood my predicament. I told her about Kim and how things had ended. She genuinely wanted to help and humored me by giving me love and affection without attachment.

It was February 2002, and it was, to say the least, unseasonably warm for February in Minnesota. I believe the high was somewhere near 70 degrees Fahrenheit. It should have been 0 degrees. Everyone walked around that warm week in disbelief. I could see people walking down the street in short sleeves, carrying heavy parkas and stocking caps in their arms, with looks of euphoric bewilderment. As a native Minnesotan, it seemed like an episode of The Twilight Zone to me. It was almost as if something strangely horrible were about to happen.

One evening, I met up with Liz at her house and we decided, since the snow had so quickly melted that week, to take a walk down to Lake Hiawatha. It was still frozen even though the temperature was in the high sixties at 6:00 PM. On the beach at dusk, we sat and talked. I couldn't sort through what to do. It was such a terrible position to be in. Liz understood.

"You're a good guy, John. You should do what makes you happy."

"But Charles."

"Charles needs a dad who is happy. John, you're not happy. Think about it."

"But I am with my son. I have to stay."

"Why?"

"Why?" It was a tough question to answer.

"Yes, why? Why do you need to stay and be miserable?"

"Because I want him to have a whole family. I have to do it for him."

"A whole family that is completely unhappy?"

I lay back on the sand and dry leaves which had fallen the previous fall and had been exposed from under the melted snow and baked in the day's sun.

I had lived by Lake Hiawatha in high school. I had collected errant golf balls and sold them back to the golfers on their way into the Hiawatha Golf Course parking lot for fifty cents apiece. Good Titleist balls that the guys would happily give a buck for three or two dollars for seven. The cops would chase me out, but I would be back a few days later, maybe at another time of day to make $20 to put towards a new microphone or blank tapes.

The girl next door was blonde and beautiful, but complicated. She was older and more experienced. We would walk down to Lake Hiawatha together some evenings. I remember sitting on a bench by the water while she studied my face.

"You have sad eyes."

"I do?"

"Yeah, they're so sad."

I thought we were connecting. Then, the next day, she was off in a Corvette with some older guy. I wished to be that experienced. Able to pick up girls. Able to think like those guys did: that she was just a chick. I longed to have that ability, that experience.

Liz lay down next to me and turned toward me, sand and leaves in her gorgeous, curly black hair. She put a hand on my face.

"You ok?"

"No. This sucks."

"Come here."

We kissed, lying in the sand facing each other. She pulled closer and pressed herself, her beautiful hips, tightly against me. It was undying physical contact. We could get together seemingly anytime and do this. It was a relationship without relationship chains. It was a seatbelt in a wreck; a mother cradling her child. It was physical contact without manipulation. That was all it was.

Sand in our hair and our clothes, we walked back. Her house was another beautiful old Minneapolis house. The immaculate hardwood stairway went up from the entryway when you walked in the front door. Her bedroom was up there. I asked to stay.

"I don't know," she said strangely, mulling the idea.

"I just want to be close. To lie next to you and sleep knowing you are there."

"That sounds nice," she started, "but I'm not the one you should do that with."

"Cindi? I guess I should."

"I don't think so. Not Cindi, John. It's Kim. You need to be with her. You should be cuddled up against her."

The words were awful. My angst returned. My soul wanted to forget, just for the night. But Elizabeth made it clear I couldn't stay. She was right. I wanted to go back to Kim, though I would not admit it to myself.

My heart was hardened.

From the Abyss   John Emil Augustine

Spring Backward

I went back to Cindi's that night. The sex began again, and I was asked to move back in. I could almost convince myself I was happy once in a while after that. I had, after all, gone from sex to sex, from Kim to Cindi, bypassing Elizabeth. I could, in my guy way, convince myself I was making a lateral move at any rate. That seemed to justify some of what I was doing. The most important part, though, was being with Charles. That was very exciting.

He had grown some, and I was happy to spend nights with him, singing him to sleep as I had once done. He enjoyed the attention, and I enjoyed giving it. I wanted him to feel more at ease, and I think he did. It was a great feeling. Paternal instinct: no one ever says it, but it exists. My new circumstance gave me a chance to share it with my boy.

I was able to be at his first birthday. Cindi's mom and her husband were in town. It was a very warm April day. Cindi and her mom bickered but were also able to join forces as well. Her mom had purchased expensive Mylar balloons and tied them to the fence outside in the yard. That's where the party was. Unfortunately, one of the strings was not tied well enough to one balloon, and with a gust of wind, it blew right off of its string.

Anyone else I knew would have said, "Well, that sucks," and gone on with the party sans one balloon. But not Cindi and her mom. They were determined to give the poor balloon guy hell until he gave them a free replacement. I remember feeling so bad for the unsuspecting guy as they both jumped in the car and sped toward his little shop. He was about to be double-teamed by hell's own dream team. He didn't stand a chance. I prayed he would give in quickly and be able to have a good day after they left. At any rate, they came back with a replacement balloon, so I was able to have a good day. At least I was on their team.

Next came Easter. My family had made brunch reservations at some restaurant. Cindi did not want to see my family. I told her not to worry and to keep a low profile: just to be quiet. Anyone who might be angry about our break-up would soon come around. After all, they were my family. And I did want Charles to be with them and with both of us. It would be good for him.

To add a bitter element to that day's plan, my grandpa had been recently diagnosed with dementia which would eventually lead to Alzheimer's. His memory was slowly going. I wanted to have some time soaking in his words of wisdom before he could no longer remember anything. I wanted to be there with him that day. It seemed Cindi understood that.

Cindi was hungry early Easter morning. She wanted a little snack to tide her over until brunch, so we drove over to the local McDonald's. On the way there she said she and Charles would not go to the brunch. I was ok with her staying home, but I insisted that Charles go.

"He has to go. It's Easter, and he will be with his family."

"I *am* his family, and he will be with *me*," she retorted.

"Listen, my grandpa isn't doing well. You know that. I want him to see and remember Charles while he can. He's crazy about Charles. Let us have some time before he forgets everything."

"I am not arguing about this, John!" she yelled.

"Oh boy," I thought, "back to this again."

My dad had given me some advice that winter. Maybe it was best used in this circumstance, I thought. When I felt myself getting pissed off, he said to just walk away. Don't hurt anyone, just walk in one direction: away. Wherever away might be, I couldn't get myself in trouble walking there.

I pulled her car into the White Castle parking lot on Lexington and University, took it out of gear, set the brake, opened the door, and walked to the stoplight on University Avenue.

Cindi got out of the car and started yelling at me as I stood there. "John! Get back here! You can't just walk away! Goddamn it, you fucker, get back here! Don't do this in front of your son! You fucking piece of shit!"

Everyone waiting at the light looked at her. It was a strange scene for a sunny Easter morning.

Then she got in the car and began to drive toward me. I walked west on University behind the Chinese restaurant and the car wash, trying to lose her. Her car screamed into the parking lots and the adjacent alley, with Charles in tow. Once in a while she would honk and yell out the window that I was an asshole. She would get out when she thought she was close enough and scream that I was ruining Easter and that I was a good for nothing mother fucking son of a bitch. I ducked behind the buildings trying to lose her. I couldn't get back into that car. I would kill her.

As I was ducking in between buildings, I noticed a squad car. And the guy inside noticed me. Soon I had two cars chasing me: Cindi's and the cop's. It was hardly fair since I was on foot! The cop easily overtook me and on went his lights.

"What's going on, guy?" the voice said from inside the car.

"I guess some domestic problems," I said, walking closer to him. "My wife is chasing me with her car. I just want to get home to my truck. I'm sorry for causing a disturbance."

"Is that her?" He pointed to her car.

"Yes. I am sorry. I don't want any trouble. I just want to get away from the situation peacefully. That's why I got out of the car. I just need to cool down, so I don't do something stupid." I was shaking. This guy could haul me in, I thought. Hauled in on Easter morning. This was just great.

But I didn't get in trouble. Instead, he asked if I needed a ride.

"I really would prefer to walk. It's just down the road."

"I understand," he said.

Woah! I thought. *A cop on my side! Was this really happening?*

He pulled away, and I took off walking toward our house. I was going to Easter brunch so long as I wasn't arrested or struck with Cindi's car.

Looking back, I saw the cop had stopped Cindi and was standing outside her car talking to her. She was waving her arms wildly. I wondered what they were saying. I figured she would get home before I would, and I would be in for a fight again. Or she would find me and hit me with her car. I walked through yards to avoid that.

When I got back, she was there but didn't come outside. I quickly walked straight up to my truck, got in, and zoomed away. I had left earlier for McDonald's in jeans and slippers and did not want to go in the house and change. But I was hardly wearing

Easter brunch attire. So I stopped at the local Kmart and bought a $10 pair of black shoes. That would have to be good enough.

When I got back home later that day, I was ready to duel. This time, I wasn't disappointed. Cindi wanted to finish the divorce. Instead, I suggested therapy. I said if we had made it this far, we could at least give it a try with someone who knew what he or she was doing. She kind of warmed up to the idea. Therapy was, after all, up her alley. She had been in and out of therapy her whole life. She even had an arrangement with her past therapist that she could call when she needed, and he would bill her under the table.

He actually had recommended that she hang a professional punching bag in the basement. I had noticed it but didn't know the purpose until that Easter afternoon. She went downstairs after we argued and beat that punching bag with a pipe for 20 minutes. This was a new one on me. I was actually a little fearful that one night she would wake me up, just briefly, with that pipe. And, to tell the truth, I thought it might be for the best.

One thing was for sure. I was back in hell where I guessed I belonged. All the things I had hated, the panic attacks, the arguments, the screaming phone calls, they all came back in full force.

But I was there for Charles, not her, so I had to look on the bright side. One nice thing about being there was the daycare. It kept her in line a bit more than before. She had to be good, or the money would stop. Jackie the doula had married her boyfriend, and their little girl, her little trick on him, was one of the kids in the daycare. Jackie and Cindi got along so well, and it was nice to see Jackie again, though less nice than I expected. I could see her doing her own conniving behind her husband's back. It was sad to overhear things she was planning and how much she disliked him. He was such a nice guy. Their little girl was adorable. But Jackie was unhappy. Truth be told, she was unhappy with herself. That I knew.

She had rigged her marriage and found out that it was not satisfying her. The minute she got what she wanted, she changed her mind. "The thought that life could be better is woven indelibly into our hearts and our brains," Paul Simon once wrote. When you plot, cheat, and trick, getting what you want can be so easy that it seems far less important when you get it. It's the American way. I got what I want, now what?

Or maybe this was part of the plan. I guess that thought crossed my mind. It was hard to tell, really. At any rate, before I knew it, the two of them, Jackie and her husband, were in court. It seemed like every month there was something that she took him to court for. On top of that sad development, Jackie had an older boy with the first guy to whom she had been married. She was in and out of court with him too. Jackie seemed to be forever fighting those two guys. It was so sad, especially for her kids. They were tugged in both directions and just looked sad all the time. I decided I would not do that. I didn't know what I would do in its place, but I wouldn't do that! Poor kids.

Meanwhile, after the daycare kids left, nights were the worst for me. I began my new habit of walking down the street to Half Time Rec, the Irish bar on Energy Park and Lexington, watching the Irish bands and drinking Guinness to kill time and brain cells. Those were such nice moments. I was out of the house. I remember one of my students even walked into the bar one time looking far sexier than she ever had in class. I had had plenty to drink that night and excused myself from a conversation to go say hi to her. She was happy to see me!

She asked me to play a game of pool. I told her I wasn't very good, but she was welcome to beat me. For a moment, I let myself believe we were on a date. I told her I could only play one game because our fraternizing was highly illegal. It reminded me of how fearful and excited I had at first been with Kim.

Kim.

I had to call her.

I excused myself after the game with my gorgeous student and went to the pay phone.

"Hello?"

"Kim?"

"Hello?"

"Kim, it's John."

"I can hardly hear you. Where are you?"

"In a bar. How are you?"

"I'm fine. What are you doing?"

"I am calling you! I love you, Kim."

"What?"

"I just called to say I love you." I sang her the line from the song for her.

"Are you drunk?"

"Yes!"

"John, I have to go."

"I love you."

"Bye."

I went back home to the couch and fell asleep.

Kim was in my dreams. We were together, doing mundane things: grocery shopping, sight-seeing, watching TV, listening to music. It was the most wonderful feeling until I woke up on the couch again. Then I knew. That reality would not grace me again. Ever.

It was at Half Time Rec a week or so later that I ran into our sax player's best friend. He was happy to see me. We had a long talk about music and what we both were up to. He asked if I had been serious the night of our final show. Would there be a new band? I told him we had thought about it, but nothing was happening right then. He immediately dialed the sax player on his cell phone and put me on after he explained we had just been talking about putting a band together. By the time I was done on the phone, we had set a date to go over a few songs that we were each working on. I figured there was no harm in swapping music.

Cindi hated that I had kept my music equipment and that it was taking up room in the basement. I would sneak down there to write very quick snippets, but she always knew and would be downstairs within a half hour yelling at me to stop it. So I worked it out with her that I would put my Hammond organ in the spare room upstairs and write there so that I could be upstairs for whatever she needed. She didn't like the idea very much, but she had to admit it was better than my being downstairs, so I got set up and began writing songs for the new band.

We would have all the old guys who still wanted to play, plus whatever fill-in guys we could find. We got both fill-in guys from the old band to play full-time with us. Then we got a ringer for a drummer, and before we knew it, we were practicing every

Wednesday night again. It was so fun and just like old times, except this time I promised myself that Cindi would not interfere with the band. I didn't care what she thought; I would not miss rehearsals or gigs. She would either adjust or be very unhappy.

In order to minimize her unhappiness, I made sure I worked on chord charts on the organ quietly at night after she was asleep, and then I would go to The Purple Onion, a Dinkytown coffee shop, and write my arrangements there during the day between grading stacks of papers. For the most part, I could do music out of her sight.

It worked out pretty well. All the arrangements and horn parts for the new band were written at The Purple Onion. It was cool to finally be able to just sit down with a pencil and crank 'em out. It gave me a lot of freedom that I hadn't had before. The charts came about much quicker than my previous trial-and-error method of writing and arranging with the old band. At least something was working out for me.

What I was realizing was that doing music was part of my nature regardless of Cindi's or anyone else's objections. I felt horribly guilty for clinging to music, but it was my only way of dealing with the world and my experiences. It always had been. Now I was able to write music and lyrics that applied to what I had gone through with Kim and Cindi. I was dealing with my loss and with trying to fit into Cindi's household once again. Music helped me understand my own feelings. It was something I could not do with a therapist, because I felt I was being judged in a therapist's office. But with my lyrics, there was no judge. Only feelings came out and could just sit there on the page no matter what anyone thought or how anyone responded to them. They were purely the plain truth as I felt and experienced it.

Cindi and I did see a couple's therapist despite my not really being very good at going to therapy. Unfortunately, she didn't help us very much. Cindi did almost all the talking. She was good at therapy. Her myriad complaints about the new band and about money and my job just spewed continually. I had made the decision to continue music, and now I was dealing with the repercussions. I can't necessarily blame Cindi for disliking my choice, either. It is hard to be a spouse of a struggling musician.

The idea of my writing and performing songs was eternally ridiculous to everyone in my family, so I can't just single Cindi out and say she alone hated my musical pursuits. It takes a special person to understand that kind of hobby and the person who obsesses over it. Today, I understand her frustration. Then, I just decided not to give her the power to destroy that part of me.

I did the same things with my lesson plans, obsessing over them. But that was different. That made money. I would get a great idea for a lesson plan and suddenly start writing. Cindi wasn't happy about my doing that, but she held her tongue. After all, the lesson plans were where the money came from. Still, she wondered if I *had* to do it at all the worst times.

I admit that I cannot control when ideas hit me. They just happen when they do. Back in those days, I was so worried I would lose the idea that I would feel compelled to do something the moment the idea came. It still sounds like I'm some sort of artistic snob when I write it that way, but that has always been how it works for me. These days, I have learned to ignore the ideas. I just end up making people angry when I act like the idea is the most important thing in the moment. Unfortunately, getting angry always went triple for Cindi.

I used to get to the therapist's office early, so I could sit in the lobby and grade papers. I tried to do everything out of Cindi's sight, so I could devote my full attention to her at home. The minute I looked like I was doing something other than what she wanted me to do, I got in trouble. Grading paper in the shrink's lobby once a week became part of my routine.

The therapist was a nice lady. She would walk past me between clients and say hello and ask me how I was doing. I suppose she thought it was weird I got there an hour or two early for our session, but it was the quietest place I had to work: no students knocking on my door, and no Cindi to bother with.

"How are you, John?" she asked one afternoon while she was making a new pot of coffee.

"Oh, I'm fine." I said matter-of-factly.

"You always say you're fine."

"I always am."

"You always are on the surface."

"Yep."

Thinking back, she probably wasn't supposed to be talking to me outside the sanctity of her office and without Cindi, but maybe she couldn't help herself. I hardly ever said anything in her office.

"You're grading papers?"

"Yeah. It's quiet here. If I do it at work, I get interrupted. If I do it at home, Cindi doesn't like it. So this actually works out great if you're not mad that I'm here early."

"Not at all."

"I'm just trying to keep everyone happy and still do my work."

"You seem to make a lot of adjustments to keep people happy."

"Naw. Not really. I made some major changes when Charles was born, and now I am just tweaking things. Trying to keep Cindi happy and still do music, for example."

"You made quite a few life changes."

"You mean when Charles was born?"

"Yes, and with Cindi."

"Sure. But I had to do what I had to do."

"You seem like you were pretty care-free before you and Cindi had Charles."

"Who wasn't before they had kids? I used to be on the road a lot before Cindi. Playing gigs. It was a lot of fun."

"Now you're a dad."

"Yeah. Kinda weird."

"You think you're making the transition ok?"

"Well I had to grow up pretty fast, if that's what you mean."

"I don't know if that was what I meant, but I understand. You did feel you had to grow up fast."

"Sure. I had to grow up like 'Bam!'" I hit my knee. "Really quick."

"But people don't just grow up quick."

"Well, I did my best. I sure didn't do anything perfectly, but I got a good job and quit music for a while. Tried to be a good dad. I've done the best I could even though it wasn't great."

"I believe you have. You actually don't strike me as the type of person who would normally go to see a therapist."

"Well I *wouldn't* normally go to see a therapist. But what else can I do? I'm trying to save my marriage. The only problem is Cindi. She's a tough sell. You've seen her. She's still not sure about me."

"I don't know that I've seen that, actually, John."

"Yeah. She wishes I were different. She gets pissed off at me. You've seen the tame version of her, I guess."

"She certainly has anger issues, yes. But that's not my role, to assess either one of you. My role is to help with the relationship."

"Do you think there is any help for this relationship?"

"Truthfully, I don't know, John."

"Well, we'll see."

"Yes, we'll see."

It was such a strange conversation. I couldn't figure out if she was trying to get me to give up or if she was trying to feel out how committed I was. It was weird. I did start to wonder if she would actually be able to help us. It almost sounded like she couldn't help. But I kept going until Cindi called it off. In the meantime, however, Cindi seemed to think the therapy was helping, so life went on somewhat normally for a little while.

Some afternoons, I would come home and play with the kids in the daycare. That was always nice because Cindi was on her best behavior around them. But one by one, each family got into it with Cindi. Each set of parents did something she didn't like. One by one she weeded them out. Jackie was first. Then it was as if I could see them all run from the daycare like the plague.

So we got a Sunday paper route to supplement her daycare income. We would go to the depot on Saturday afternoon, stuff the papers with all the ads, then wake up at about 1 AM Sunday morning, load Charles into my truck, and take off. By 5 AM we were done, and the day dragged by after that. Still, what we made was enough to fix our money predicament.

Most of the time, Charles slept soundly while we delivered, but I remember one morning he was crying, and we couldn't do anything but finish as quickly as possible. But his crying really made Cindi crazy. At some point, she told me to move over and let her drive. I was too slow. So we hot-rodded through the neighborhoods. Then we got a flat. She was fuming.

I jumped out and began to change the tire with Charles still crying inside and Cindi standing over me, swearing and working herself into a frenzy. She kept yelling at me to go faster. Finally, I stood up and said, "You want faster? Be my guest." And dumped the tools on the ground.

That really got her going, and she fumbled with the nuts and the jack. She was so worked up that she shook uncontrollably. By time she slowly and clumsily finished, she was wild. She yelled at the top of her lungs, "*Get in the fucking truck!*" as I was putting the tools back. It was at that moment that I decided I would never go along with her again to deliver papers. I kept quiet and helped her finish, and then I told her that had been my last time.

She was beyond furious. I just said, "Hey, this is your baby now. I don't need that kind of treatment. You go ahead and do it yourself. You're so fast and so good at it, so I'll stay out of your way."

That was not the right thing to say, and I could picture that pipe, as she swung it madly against the punching bag in the basement, hitting my head while I slept.

But it didn't matter. I was finished anyway, regardless.

From the Abyss   John Emil Augustine

Knock Outs and Knock Offs

I had taken to spending the few hours before our rehearsals every Wednesday afternoon at BJ's on Broadway and Highway 94 in North Minneapolis. To begin with, I always drank at a bar before the rehearsals. Then one day I was sitting there thinking, "I could be doing this *and* looking at naked chicks. What am I, stupid?"

So that day I finished my drink, drove to BJ's a few miles from our jam spot, and thus began my Wednesday afternoon ritual. I was often the youngest guy in the bar. The girls liked me. I didn't care. I knew I was too poor for them to really like me. Though I did end up dating one of the girls for a while, mostly just to say I had done it. I never had sex with her, though, because that prospect scared me.

I actually liked and was friends with several of the girls. They were quite pleasant, though I eventually understood why each of them was doing what she did. There was something a little off with each girl. Still, when one of the girls came around, in a small bottom and even smaller or no top, and asked if I wanted a private dance, I would slap $20 down on the bar and say, "Just have a drink with me." The dance didn't interest me. I paid for one once, but I wasn't allowed to touch her. That wasn't fun at all, it was torture!

One of the girls (and I have no idea anymore what her name was) always pushed my $20 back to me and sat and talked anyway. She was a knock-out. She was fit. Her boobs weren't huge but perfectly round and beautiful: real boobs, not implants. I still love real boobs, and at the time, I loved all the differences in the girls at BJ's. They were all beautiful in different ways. The knock-out was otherwise gorgeous as well. She was tan and had dark hair and an interesting nose: a little crooked, but it added to her charm. She had a little Italian in her. She even had a widow's peak; that was pretty hot in itself. Her eyes were brown, her lips were lush, and her thin hips and smooth back were wonderful. I remember telling her that it was so nice to be around her.

"Yeah, it's nice to have someone who listens, I know."

"Kinda, but I'm not stupid. I know you're just killing time until your next set."

She had no response.

"I don't mind. I think you're cool anyway. But what I really like, I am finding, is the proximity of a naked girl. You're not screaming at me, and you're gorgeous. Those two things are so relaxing, even if for just a few hours a week. Seriously, your proximity puts my mind at ease." I don't think she got it, and I'm sure she went home and screamed at her poor boyfriend plenty. But just like Cindi, while she was on the job, she was pleasant. She had to be.

BJ's was truly a respite, shitty as it was. It was a knock-off version of paradise or at least the best version I had at the moment. There was one girl there I liked best of all. She was blonde and curvy. She had a sly smile, and she was smart. She reminded me so much of Kim, though her face wasn't as cute. She was forward, too. She would always come up to me at the bar and ask if I wanted a dance, after having danced on stage, twisting her hips this way and that, staring in my eyes the whole time. I always ended up giving her $20 to sit with me for a little bit, and she always took the $20. I didn't care. She was wonderful, like Kim. Well, not really, but I had to settle for this expensive knock-off. Really, it was the best I could hope for.

Every Wednesday night, I came home smelling of booze, smoke, and perfume, but I didn't care. I washed my clothes and took a shower and waited until the next Wednesday when I would go back to that dirty, disgusting, fake version of paradise. But the girls there, they could not be hurt, nor could they hurt me. Anything I said didn't matter, and I could never mess up or let them down. They were immune.

One Saturday morning in August, the heat hadn't picked up yet, and Cindi and I had the windows open and the fans blowing in the cool morning air. We would need it later when the day heated up. And this day was about to heat up and blow.

It was always the same. Every weekend, the same fight occurred. She wanted a divorce. The therapist couldn't do anything for us. She was just an expensive chair warmer. Cindi was nothing but angry. The anger oozed out, no matter what anybody said to her. You can't talk the anger out of someone, and Cindi was hopelessly mired in it. She often seemed like The Creature from the Abyss; a great big slimy thing in a rumpled and wrinkled cardboard cave on the silver screen. Luring her out just exasperated the situation and made her mean, particularly when I was involved. Therapy was hopeless. We ended up just yelling in the therapist's office every week. It was a ridiculous waste of money when we could yell at each other at home for free.

That morning, we yelled back and forth while Charles sat in his high chair eating Cheerios. I just kept thinking how bad for him this constant, cruel arguing was. This whole scene seemed a waste. Cindi, however, loved it. She was in her element, snapping off the trees like they were bonsai ornaments on a dry-wobble landscape

"This is *it*, John!"

"Fine, this is it. See ya."

"Good! Get out!"

"I'm not the one who's leaving."

"Fuck you! *Get out of my house!*"

"You're leaving, Cindi. You're the problem, and you're about to be escorted out."

"Is that a threat, John?"

This had become our usual conversation. But this time, looking at Charles sitting there soaking this all in, I decided that this was, in fact, it.

I grabbed both her arms, and she struggled to free herself. But she wasn't strong enough for all the adrenaline that had built up over time. I knew I should walk away. My dad was right. Nonetheless, she was about to leave.

"*You're hurting me, you asshole!*" She pushed against me, struggling against my movement toward the living room.

"You are about to leave, you bitch," I growled. It was a new sound. Something I never did but of which I was quite capable.

This caught her off guard. She froze as I pushed her through the dining room, through the living room, and onto the porch. Then I slammed and locked the front door, ran to the back, and locked that door too.

I stood next to Charlie's highchair and realized why a guy could be inclined to beat his wife. This was why. I could have twisted her neck and broke her spine at that moment. That's how enraged I was. Standing there, the full force of adrenaline pumping through my body, it suddenly scared me. I scared myself. This was why my dad had given me that advice, to walk away. One swing of my fist could knock Cindi out cold. I knew I was capable of it. I wouldn't have to think about it. I could just let my body do what it naturally wanted to do. The thought froze me. I had fought this urge the whole relationship.

While I remained frozen in thought, Cindi had gone to the kitchen window, ripped off the screen, and climbed in. At that moment, I knew I was beaten. I was either about to go to prison for the rest of my life or leave. That was what it boiled down to. I backed up and let her take Charles out of his highchair. She took him upstairs, and to ease my own mind, I followed her to see if she would kill him. That's all I was worried about. She was as pissed as I was.

But she sat down in the chair and rocked him, saying, "Shhhhhh," over and over. When I came into the room, she said, "Get the fuck away from me."

"Are you going to hurt him?"

"I am not going to hurt him."

"I have your word. You will not hurt him."

"I will not fucking hurt him, John."

And with that, I was gone.

It seemed to me, metaphorically or literally, either her pipe or my adrenaline would deliver the knock-out blow were we to continue down the path we were on. One way or another, it would only get uglier. The ugliness was something I could not model for my son. I could not, in good conscience, cross that line. Perhaps I already had, but stopping now was in his best interest. I had failed. Twice. I was unable to out-swim the shark. I was unable to read the sign. I was too dumb to know the one-person relationship was a ridiculous pipe dream. The sign on the pipe suddenly hit me. One person making all the relationship sacrifices and compromises for the other? Utterly ridiculous.

There it was: the sign I could never read and had always missed. I could not be strong enough for both of us. I could not be compassionate enough for both of us. I could not out-last the heat if I were the one stoking the fire, intentionally or unintentionally. I could not be my own good relationship. I could not make someone change. I can't tell you what a spiritual knock-out it was for me to realize that. I was thoroughly and completely beaten. The blow was devastating.

In my optimistic way, I had completely dismissed the "I can't" statements. If I worked harder, did more, was more, I could accomplish anything. I knew this to be true. The possibilities were endless. The limitations could be overcome…*always!* That was my belief. Nothing was too great a task for me. I had stamina, I had hope, I had courage, and I could dream anything. All I had to do was to make my dream a reality with hard work and commitment. These things I believed with every ounce of my being and every molecule within me. The signs that said, "You can't do this all by yourself," may as well have been written in Martian. Those words were irrelevant to me. They were an utter lie, in fact. Nothing could have been farther from the truth, to me, than the words, "You can't."

But I couldn't.

I never lived in that house again.

From the Abyss   John Emil Augustine

Aimlessness

I had lost my family, and losing my family was more traumatic than I think I realized at the time. I began a downward spiral. Once the divorce actually happened, I was lost. I kept asking myself, "How could this have happened to me?" as if I had somehow caused all this. I kept wondering what was wrong with me. I had no idea my feelings were that of a normal person in an abnormal situation. In court that spring, I gave Cindi as much as the judge would let me. We signed the papers, and I was out.

Other than having the new band, I was aimless for a while. Ammon, our trombone player, and his girlfriend let me move in with them at Roland's house. Roland was in Michigan with his wife while she did her residency, and Ammon was taking care of the place. The new bass player lived there too. I was right back to where I'd started except I had a son and an ex-wife.

Every night at Roland's, we sat on the front porch: drinking, toking, and laughing uncontrollably. One night, we decided our house would make a great setting for a sit com. We debated various episode possibilities and even came up with a theme song in a cheesy 80s rock shuffle:

> *I'm a single dad*
> *(And we're his buddies)*
> *They just hang around*
> *(We ain't got no money)*
> *And...neither do I*

When you're stoned, it's hilarious, and laughter was the medicine I needed.

Still, the best medicine, a stable relationship, eluded me. The entire summer of 2003, I wished with all my heart that I could get back together with Kim. I finally got up my nerve and wrote her in August, but she had a new boyfriend and was not receptive. Not only that, but I assumed she hated my guts, and I did not blame her one bit.

Even so, after a few emails in September, I decided to write her and tell her to meet me at Uncommon Grounds in Uptown, just down the road from her new apartment.

It was October. The air was cooling once again. I was about to face another winter alone and void of love. I suppose I should have been used to it, but the pain was approaching anyway. Before the lonely winter, I needed to voice something that weighed heavily on my mind. I had to talk to Kim. I told her I would be at the coffee shop whether she came or not but asked her please not to let me down.

She didn't. That was the strange pull I had on her. She would not let me down.

"Kim, I don't want anything to come of this, but I had to tell you face-to-face."

"John, I have a boyfriend. We can't get back together. I already told you."

"I don't want to get back together. I want you to love your boyfriend."

She was quiet. It was a cool fall night. The lighted cars on Hennepin Avenue went by the front patio. We sat on the chilly metal chairs in coats. Colorful leaves outlined the patio stones and twittered in the occasional breeze.

"John, I have to get back."

"I have to tell you I love you, Kim. I will always love you."

"What do you want me to do with that?"

"Nothing."

"Nothing? You must want something."

"I want things to be the way they are, but I could not go on knowing I didn't take every possible chance to say, I love you."

"That's it?"

She was so pretty. Why couldn't I have seen it? Why had I left her? We could be cuddled up on our couch watching a movie or talking about our wedding. No, I had to stop thinking that as I sat, looking at her beautiful blonde hair, a curl gently waving in the wind.

"That's it."

"John, you can't keep doing this. Please tell me you will not do this again."

"I won't."

"John." She sighed. "What am I going to do with you?"

"Walk away."

"That's what you *had* to tell me. You love me and want me to walk away?"

"That's all."

"You are so weird!"

"I am sorry, and I know I am weird. I am sorry to be weird."

"Uh! John!" She just looked at me.

"I don't want you or me to do anything. I just needed you to know after all the horrible things I did, that I didn't mean them, and I didn't mean to hurt you."

"John! You did hurt me, and it's over."

"I know I did, Kim. I know what I am, and I am not happy about it. But if there ever was any question, please know that I love you."

"Don't keep saying that."

"I'm done."

We drank our tea in silence.

Then she walked into the night.

From the Abyss   John Emil Augustine

Hitting Bottom

My Wednesday ritual at BJ's had become a semi-nightly ritual. The more often I went, the more I began to find the Rum and Cokes had less of an effect on me. The girls had less of an effect, too. I noticed myself not even looking at the stage. I would walk into the dim smoke cloud, go directly to the men's room by the front door and piss in the urinal while the slush from the parking lot melted off my boots. Then I would walk up to the bar, looking at no one, find a good spot on the corner, hang my jacket on the chair, and order a Jack and Coke. Jack was more potent than rum.

    I would sit and joke with Troy the bartender, who I knew from the Cabooze. He loved going out with the dancers, and he was good at the chase. He loved flirting and having them over to his house for parties. I went to a few but could not drum up the interest he had in that scene. Troy went through several girls during the time I knew him, and I always wondered what he wanted from them. It seemed like such a futile enterprise to me, anyway, dating the dancers. What was the point of that kind of romance? Sex? I couldn't imagine the consequences of sex with some of those girls.

    However, I could imagine the consequences of dating them, because I saw them in Troy: drama, heartbreak, uncomfortable work situations, late nights, and lots of drugs and booze. He looked continuously and increasingly tired. The relationships seemed so hopeless, yet he was locked into the cycle for some reason. We even wrote a song about it together one night at the bar: "She's Got a Smile." It was kind of a Johnny Cash sounding song. Roland was in town, so I had him lay down guitar and bass tracks over what I had recorded, and then I gave a copy to Troy. He really liked it. It was cool to see how proud he was of that little song. The lyrics went like this:

> *She's got a smile that says so well*
> *That life is kind, so just unwind*
> *Don't make it hell*

From the Abyss John Emil Augustine

She says it's all right
She says, "Tell me what you need
Because the two of us just clicked
Suddenly and softly here tonight."

I had a dream we were lying in her bed one night
Listening to the rain gently fall
Nothing to do but fuck, cook, and talk awhile
No one but you and me and the walls

But the closer I get, the worse she looks
And she complains and she's got pains
And I found I mistook
Her tricks for beauty
And I could try to make it work
Or I could walk away now
And I don't even know which one would suit me

I had a dream we were lying in her bed one night
She sang those B Sides tunes like she does
But I woke up on the floor among the bottles and the haze
Just trying to figure out whose floor it was

I guess it's kind of depressing when I read it now. But that was life. The drinks didn't numb me enough after a while, so I took to smoking a joint in my truck before entering the bar, then getting many Jack and Cokes. That did it pretty well. I would stay out very late, drive home completely messed up, and lay down in my bed.

The best thing I could do was hold perfectly still when I made it to bed. Were I to become uncomfortable and roll over, I knew I was about to go through real hell. The minute I made the choice to move, the room would begin to spin. What a horrible feeling. I knew it would be all over after that. I could hold as still as I wanted in that new position, but the spinning would not stop. Inevitably, I would totter to the door of my room that led to the deck, or I would crawl if I could not stand, then I would get as close to the edge of the deck as I could and puke. Eventually, I attached the garden hose to the railing so that in the morning I could hose down my normal spot on the deck. It was a disgusting existence.

More and more often the other guys would be having a house party when I got back with my bag of White Castles after my late night at BJ's. I began to hate the people who came over regardless of whether I knew them or not. I have vague memories from that time. I remember peeing when I got home one time and just wondering how I could ever be sober. It felt so great to be ripped. Sober was reality. Why would I ever want to go back to that? I remember barely making it up to my room one night and collapsing onto the bed. I couldn't move. I felt almost comatose. A girl stumbled through my door, across my room, and fell on my chair and TV table in the corner, completely bending the table. Then she stumbled out again. I remember little scenes like that.

The house was always smoky. I kept my bedroom door closed, so the smoke would not get in and affect Charles when he slept there, but it was clear to Cindi when she picked him up that the house was not a great place for a kid. I began having him go to my folks' on weekends to keep him out of the house. But my time there was wearing thin.

I normally brought Charles to my parents' house on weekends, because I didn't want him staying with me at the house. It was becoming less and less a place for a kid. One girl actually broke my roommate's window when no one was home. She broke in because he owed her money. Ammon came home to find her running around our house half-crazed. That was when I realized it was time to stop bringing Charles over.

Unfortunately (or fortunately), one weekend in March my folks were out of town, so I brought Charles over to the house against my better judgment. Saturday night went fine. It was a quiet night in the house. But when Cindi came over to pick him up Sunday afternoon, she did not like the vibe of the house.

When she walked in, she sniffed the air. "Has someone been smoking in here?" She asked. It was a fair question.

"We smoke during rehearsals on Wednesdays," I lied. We smoked in the basement all the time. Not when Charles was there: that was my rule. But we smoked plenty otherwise. With the house shut up for the winter, the stale smoke smell was always a presence.

"I don't like this," she said, looking around. "Something doesn't feel right about this house."

Boy, had she nailed it. I remember sitting down on the piano bench in the dining room. Enormous tears unexpectedly formed in my eyes. I suppose it was a combination of being cornered and knowing I would now be asked to give up my time with Charles. I just couldn't hold in the sadness.

"John, what is going on?"

"I know it's not a great place. That's why I go to my folks' on the weekends. I don't know what else to do."

"Why don't you move?"

"I can't afford it."

"I don't think I can let Charles come here anymore."

"No. Actually, I wouldn't either." More tears silently formed.

"So what? You don't want to see him?"

"I want to see him. Of course."

"Then move."

"Where?"

"Well, I could probably help you find a place. Why don't you move closer to me, so you don't have to drive so far?"

"Uhh," I sighed heavily. "How am I going to do that? I only pay $500 a month here." I wiped my eyes with my hand.

"I'm sure you could get a place for seven or eight."

"Yeah?"

"You can handle that, can't you?"

"I have no idea."

"Well, I think you will have to make it work. *This* isn't going to work anymore. Not for Charles, anyway."

"Yeah. I guess I will start looking."

"I will too. We'll find something."

A family who had a child at her daycare knew of a four-plex on their block with an $800 a month apartment for rent. It was a one-bedroom with a kitchen, a dining room which I used as a studio, a living room, a bathroom, and a sun room where I put Charles's toys. The wood floors were to be kept pristine, so I put rugs everywhere. The plaster and paint were peeling in the corners by the woodwork, but the place would work ok for Charles and me. Since Cindi was on my side at the time, I had her come with me to view the apartment, so she could pick out things she didn't like and lay into my new landlord. It was a bad decision on my part because Cindi just ended up not liking the place, and the landlord just ended up not liking Cindi.

The apartment wasn't perfect, but it really was in good shape for my needs. It was clean, and the water and stove worked fine. The radiators kept the place warm in the winter, so what else could I want? The cosmetic problems were nothing to me.

Once I was settled, Charles was able to sleep over twice a week. Those nights, we had so much fun, and it was great to be able to have that time with him. My landlord, a nice older lady who kept the place up while the owners lived in Europe, told me she loved to hear Charles while I gave him a bath in the evenings. She told me it was so much fun for her to hear him laughing and splashing. I felt bad we were so noisy, but she told me that was the one place the sound carried, and she didn't mind. She thought it was great the way we interacted. It was too. It was a heck of a lot of fun.

The nights he wasn't there were awful. I would drink at least a six-pack, smoke at least two bowls, and also smoke a pack of cigarettes outside between the time I got home and the time I went to sleep. There was no other way to sleep without those aids. I had such a horrible weight hanging over my head.

I often thought about Kim. In my stupor, I wished she would find me somehow. I wished I had not blown two chances: my family with Cindi and my life with Kim. Thinking about Kim was heartbreaking if I had not smoked enough pot, so I made sure to always have a stash in the apartment. Each night without Charles, I would light my make-shift aluminum foil bowl, blow the smoke out through a paper towel tube stuffed with dryer sheets, and all my negative thoughts would drift far away.

Inevitably, they would come back. If not that night, the next day. I would dwell on them and try to devise plans to get Kim back, to get into her heart somehow. I wrote songs for her. What did it matter? She would never hear them. She would never know. One went like this:

Curly or straight
Sometimes I couldn't wait
To be surprised
I'd look away from your door
Hoping you'd be there before
I focused my eyes

Night's cold in December I will
Think of your smile
All alone in the darkness I will
Think of you for a while
Night's cold
I think of you
Night's cold
I think of you

Hungry or sad
Somehow you always had
Sunshine for me
But I don't want
A memory that haunts me
And will never leave

Night's cold this December I might
Think of your smile
All alone in the darkness I'll try not to
Think of you for a while
Night's cold
I think of you
Night's cold
I think of you

Cindi took me to court again for more money. Since I was already strapped with our credit card debt, my student loan debt, and my divorce lawyer debt, I was forced to move out of my apartment in December 2004. I didn't move anywhere, I just became homeless. The apartment was my single biggest expense, and the only way to pay all the other expenses was to eliminate an apartment altogether. I put in my notice with my November rent check, and by January first, that was that.

It was cold living in my truck in January. I hated doing that. It was cramped trying to sleep across two bucket seats, my head propped in the driver's seat and my hip wedged in the passenger seat with the seat belt stuck in my side every night. No matter how I tried to shove it out of the way, it would work its way back to the same spot under my ribs. On a very cold night, I would turn the truck on until it got too hot, wake up, turn the truck off until it got too cold, wake up again, and turn it back on. I repeated that all night. All the while, I would twist and turn; trying to find a comfortable position.

Sleep was becoming more and more elusive. Sometimes I stayed a night here or there at a friend's house. I hated so much to be in that situation, to have to be the loser friend who asked to stay over for the night because I was sleeping in my truck. It reminded me again of the joke about the keyboardist. Except now I had no girlfriend.

Somehow my situation came up with my buddy, Jake, and his wife when we were having lunch. His wife insisted I stay in their guest bedroom. So for a few months, they put me up. The night I moved in, it was my 30th birthday. I can't describe what a good present it was to have such a nice room and bed in which to sleep.

That night, it just so happened they were pulling up their carpet. Apparently, the installers had messed up a seam, and it was right in a very visible place. I think the company had agreed to redo the carpet, but they would charge to pull it up, so I helped them, and we made fairly short work of the job. I remember thinking how remote the problem of a visible carpet seam felt to me. At the time, I didn't think anything could get better than just having a bed. And now not to have to see a carpet seam when I came downstairs; it was pretty luxurious.

Still, it was a bittersweet birthday. I had a place to sleep with friends, and I was able to help them with a little project that night. That amounted to two good feelings, and I was thankful for that much. But not to detract from their project, I didn't tell them it was my birthday. So my 30th was the first time in my life my birthday wasn't observed by anyone. That was a little sad, but I couldn't help but be happy in a house with my friends. I just pretended it wasn't my birthday.

In my friends' house, I was able to quit doing a few things because they just didn't do them: drugs, cigarettes, and heavy drinking. It's amazing what you can do given the right environment. They had no need for weed or cigarettes. Normally in the evenings, I would have smoked up, drank a six pack, and smoked an entire pack of cigarettes. But out of respect, I didn't do any of that stuff.

Jake and I would always have a beer or two together at the end of the day while his wife had a glass of wine but not like I had been drinking, not in that quantity. In addition, while living there, the idea of going to a strip club disgusted me. In fact, I never went again. I didn't want to come home to their nice house hammered and puke anywhere on the premises. It seemed so disrespectful that I just couldn't do it.

I found that my friends' existence, though it could be chaotic at times, was far more peaceful than the one I had come to know. I longed for the kind of peacefulness that I saw modeled. While I lived there, I reaped the benefits of rehab and retraining. In the end, it was a great 30th birthday gift, and they didn't even know they had given it to me.

I lived with them for just two short months, from March to May. Sober again, it was time to move on.

The Beautiful Moon

I sit in the warehouse where I work today, waiting for the next truck to come in and thinking of all this. I've now been married six years and have four boys including Charles. I have been laid off from teaching for five years. My alcohol intake has become about one beer a night, if that. My wife is so patient, so good at managing all the crap I've had dumped on my soul as a result of my getting my butt kicked in my first marriage. I am very lucky in that respect. I am also lucky I was taught to accept her help, to accept the notion that I am not in this by myself, to be able to receive love in addition to giving it.

    I have overcome a lot in between then and now. I have had to hit bottom several times since. A little like the forklift I had to learn to operate, the one sitting idly directly in front of me on the cement floor, any amount of instruction could not equal the hard knocks I had to go through while learning to drive it. I have run it into the racks dozens of times. I've dropped product off the shelves, have hit and broken lights with the mast. I know I still will make some rookie mistakes. In a way, some of the dumb mistakes I will make will keep me in check, keep my head from getting too big. I can't do everything on that forklift, even if I think I can.

    I've been told by one of my mentors in life, the kind of teacher who just seems to appear at the right moment, that I have many lessons ahead of me. She is always able to pin-point exactly what is happening with me. If you listen, you might hear someone like this in the wind, someone who is there to help you along too. At any rate, I have no doubt that I have much ahead of me to endure, perhaps more than is behind me. Fear is in the unknown, but I become less fearful as I go. After all, we are just people and can either be afraid of each other or can accept that there will always be adversity and work together to overcome it. How you react is what your children will learn and use later in their own lives with others. We have to learn, and we also have to turn around and teach. And we have to learn that there are instances in which we cannot teach. There are people who have not yet and perhaps never will learn, who are stuck in their own lessons and cannot see the signs. Sometimes we have to know to let those people be.

Cindi is one of those people, and she still threatens my family and me. I still go to court at her request, but I have stopped listening to the accusations. I know what she says about me is a way to manipulate, to bully me into getting something. That something always involves money. If necessary, we have court-appointed people come to our house and interview our family because she has made up something about us. It can take a lot of screwing around on our and the court's part for someone to eventually say my family isn't even close to as bad as we were made out to be. We know. But they have to check it out. It reminds me of my great-grandma, always angling and conniving to get something for herself, telling the nurses at the home stories about my grandpa which he would then have to defend against, because she wanted to order some wonder dish cloth from TV.

But there is only so much money. Cindi can have some. Charles is entitled to it, and I want him to have as much as I can give so long as that does not put the rest of the family in jeopardy. Money is necessary for survival, but when it becomes a goal, as it is to Cindi, then survival becomes secondary, and money's achievement becomes primary. It changes a person. Things are done without the least concern for anyone else; things which, in the end, can only backfire.

We can't take the money with us. I don't care who you are. The Koch brothers are going to die just like the rest of us, and then what? What privileges will either of them have? Privilege is an illusion. None of us is any more privileged than the other. We are all miserable or ecstatic depending on how we go through our day, how we view each other and ourselves.

"A Zen Master lived the simplest kind of life in a little hut at the foot of a mountain. One evening, while he was away, a thief sneaked into the hut only to find there was nothing in it to steal. The Zen Master returned and found him. 'You have come a long way to visit me,' he told the prowler, 'And you should not return empty handed. Please take my clothes as a gift.' The thief was bewildered, but he took the clothes and ran away. The Master sat naked, watching the moon. 'Poor fellow,' he mused, 'I wish I could give him this beautiful moon'" (Zen Stories to Tell Your Neighbors, John Suler, Ph.D.).

We can forget that we are here to learn. We sometimes think we are here to consume, to manipulate our way to a better position in life. Then we consume and manipulate ourselves right out of business. Everyone we've cheated to get the dumb things we want will no longer back us up. Everyone we were a monster to will say, "See ya later." We know these people. They are friendless, and all it takes for someone new is a little time before they get the idea that that person is poison.

There's a lot of poison on the earth. I see on the news and Facebook postings that we will no longer tolerate bullying. I understand the purpose of calling attention to the problem, but the problem is deeper than what we can call attention to. Trying to take the ass and the hole out of an asshole is a completely separate problem from fighting the resulting action once he or she has become a bully.

I describe Cindi to my younger kids like this. Everybody has two parts inside them: a good part and a bad part. The two parts have to work together, and we need them both.

"We need a bad part?" they ask, confused.

I say, "Yes. The part of you that is mean to your brother, the bad part, is important too. It needs to be there. But the bad part needs to learn how to work together with the good part. The good part will teach the bad part when to be mean. They need to be a team.

"Most of the time, the good part is in charge, and the bad part learns to take cues from the good part. When the good part is having trouble with, let's say, someone being mean to you, the good part wakes the bad part up and says, 'Hey, I need your help.' The bad part gets up and is strong. It is in-your-face. It will not let your good part get pushed around. The bad part is necessary.

"Once the bad part is done, the good part has to calm it down a little and say, 'Thanks, bad part, I've got it from here.' They have to be friends for the trade-off to work. They have to work together, and that takes some trial-and-error; it takes practice. But the cues have to come from the good part. If the bad part starts giving the cues, things get messed up inside a person."

My little ones have witnessed Cindi. They have seen her bad part in action. It is horrifying to them. But they have also seen her acting nice, and it's hard for them to know whether she is nice or mean. They say, "She is nice now." I have to tell them not to be fooled. I have to explain her like this. Her bad part is in charge of her good part. She has had so many threats in her life that the bad part has had to take over for survival's sake. Her bad part has had to stand up for her good part a lot. But as a normal person would have their good part take back the reins at some point, when hers has taken over, something bad has happened again, and the bad part has realized that with its guard down, the good part will be taken advantage of over and over.

So at some point, the good part just had to take the backseat. The bad part had to say, "From now on, I'm in charge." Since then, the sword has permanently been out; the armor has always been up; the dog has always been ready to bite. Unfortunately, the bad part eventually just makes people back away. When you make everyone back off, you find out you struggle to keep a job, for example, because no one wants to work with you. So that survival method gets you away from danger, but it also gets you away from people who you need for the other aspects of survival.

Cindi's bad part was not willing to let the good part win people over, because that would mean letting down its guard. So the bad part had to learn how to act like the good part. It wouldn't be able to do it forever, because acting good was against its nature, but it could pull it off for short amounts of time. The bad part really learned to mimic the good part well after a while. That's what, I explain to my little ones, they are seeing when Cindi is being nice. Her bad part is pretending to be good. Even though it is not exactly her fault, as she is probably not aware of it, we still have to be careful and remember exactly what is going on inside of her and not expect the bad part to be able to pretend to be good forever. Eventually, something will happen to make the bad part act badly. We have to be careful not to trust the bad part, especially when it is being nice.

It's a very sad circumstance, particularly knowing what my kids have experienced and knowing why they need to have such things explained. At the same time, we are getting at the heart of bullying from our perspective. We are getting at what abuse is and how to deal with it beyond simply recognizing it. Our society will get there too, but we have to know that there will always be circumstances that produce those who are instigators. Encountering these circumstances at a young age, having time to process under calm direction, and being able to practice responding may help. More than that, one's outlook helps quite a bit more. After all, can we be a victim of a lesson? My answer is that we can only be victimized by a life lesson if we do not learn what we are meant to. Once you learn the lesson, you are not a victim at all. Not any more than you were victimized by learning to write. You are victimized by all the red marks on your high school papers until you realize that they didn't really matter in the "grand scheme." Doing poorly only means that you were doing. You can always improve something that didn't come out perfectly the first or even the twentieth time. When you lean that, you are no longer a victim. You are the victor!

The way you view someone who instigates makes a difference, too. You can fight, but for what? For a short time you may need to, but for a prolonged time, you just end up pumping poison into your own body. You fight and fight, using the part of yourself that fights, until all you know is fighting. All that exists is the part that fights. You have been poisoned. You will never win with that poison coursing through your body. You will never defeat anyone but yourself. In essence, you will become Cindi, always scheming, always up in arms and spewing poison to those who have shrugged their shoulders and walked away.

Poor Cindi. I can't give her the beautiful moon. Perhaps someone can but not me. I have accepted that.

The floor is dirty here in the warehouse. The days can be long and tiring. The work can be mind-numbing. Once in a while as I sit here waiting for a truck to pull into the dock, I think back to when I taught. I could go back. I won't get into the details, but I could get back into it. If so, I would do it only for the students, because I loved my students. I would, if I could, forget all the politics and who liked or disliked my teaching practices, and I would concentrate solely on the students, because in the end, they were what mattered. I wanted them to come away with a positive experience from learning. That's what we should all come away from life with, as life is just one learning experience after another. Some of us have more, some have fewer, but we all have them. We should position ourselves to have positive outcomes; to come out the victor of a lesson, not the victim.

The experience depends upon you. No one can force you to have a positive experience or a positive outlook. I could hate this place. I could hate the drivers as they come in. I could hate the bean counters who don't think I'm worthwhile enough to give me more money. But where would that get me? I'd start dwelling on either getting more money or on my anger at not having enough money.

My kids don't care about that. They want a dad who is good to them and is fun to be around. They want a dad from whom they can learn. They want to be able to enjoy the beautiful moon with me. I believe it is my purpose, as far as they are concerned, to show them that how you look at a thing determines your reality. Nothing is going to go exactly as you have planned. In the end, the plan doesn't really matter. What matters is how you treat those around you, how your good part and your bad part work together, how you handle yourself in adversity, what you learn from each lesson, and how you pass on your knowledge and wisdom.

I look at the warehouse floor. It needs sweeping. Maybe a wash. A few orders have come in, and it is time to prepare them to be shipped this afternoon. This is not a dull life by any means. This is not slavery. I am not chained to this. Each act in itself is life. I perform each simply and happily. I have something to do. Doing is its own simple reward: to perform a task, to simply do. There is no difference in recording a song. While I lay down each track, I am completely in the task, in the moment. Each vibrating string of my mandolin, each thud of the bass drum is life. Each action of my hand or foot is a simple motion which I perform completely and happily. I am with the song in my studio as I am with the broom here in the warehouse.

Listening to the track is joy. A clean floor is joy. This, today, is joy. This is heaven: each motion, each moment. This is a paradise. No need to wish for something which, when it comes, will not be enough again. No need to fight to get on to the next thing thinking, finally I will be happy. In fact, this floor which needs sweeping, this broom, this dust pan, will make me happy because I will be completely with the moment. I am here doing. The typing of these words, the revision of these words – I am completely in it and have no need to seek better words or a better story. I have been and am now with the story, completely.

The beauty of this outlook is that it doesn't make you a zombie stuck on mundane tasks pretending you are happy. I know it sounds like that. However, I could be as happy sweeping the floor as I could be running the company. There is no ambition eliminated; quite the opposite, in fact. You realize that when you are completely with your life, you find your real passions and act on them. When you find something that you want deeply, you truly relish every part of reaching that goal. You enjoy the process.

Your life is a process to be enjoyed.

However, this outlook doesn't make you enjoy a bad relationship. It makes you appreciate the good ones and learn from the bad ones. When you are truly with the bad relationship, you can understand what makes it bad, and you can learn from it. You may not necessarily enjoy the process at the time, and it would make sense that you would not enjoy something negative, were you truly in it with your entirety. But knowing there is a lesson, at least at the end of the episode, you are truly with learning. You are truly with your life.

Otherwise, you are in denial. You cannot be in denial and be engrossed in the events of your life. That is impossible. You cannot pretend to be something and also be it in reality. Once you are actually being, there is no more pretending. Once you are pretending, you are not being. After all, had I not gotten to this state of mind, I would still be angry and depressed about all of this. I could not pretend my way around being angry and hurt. I am either angry and hurt, or I am not.

In that case, the lesson, rather than being a positive one, would simply be unhappily unlearned. Then I could not write any of this. Who would read my list of complaints? It would be a non-story, a non-lesson. Being truly with the story, I am able to see the paradise that is still my life, regardless of others' misdoings, regardless of others' actions, though they affect me still. Why poison myself and believe I am suffering? Am I? At the moment, I am content to type all of this for you. Oh, how I could pretend to be suffering! Oh, I am suffering still, I would say. I have learned nothing, I would say. You would read that whether I literally wrote it or not. You would read the bullshit between the lines, and my story would be irrelevant to almost any reader. Am I suffering? Once in a while, sure. I am still learning, after all. Then I learn, and the suffering turns to happiness, and the paradise is that much richer. I know it will happen as I go into the lesson, so the fear of the lesson is far less harsh. I don't fear enduring this life. I look forward to it. I can take the crap out of my paradise for myself as only Kim could do for me once upon a time.

We are taught to believe that some great paradise, a heaven, is waiting for us at the end of our suffering on earth. There is no proof or disproof of this notion; faith is required. However, I know I have proven, at least to myself, that there is a paradise right here, right now, in the ticking of my keyboard keys. In the roar of the Volvo tractor and trailer as it pulls up to the dock; in the buzz of my didgeridoo when I get home. This is not suffering. This is not the horrid test we have been led to believe we must endure to pass from this life to the next. This is the next. Why wouldn't it be? This, right here, right now, is heaven. We are told we do not have the capacity to know heaven, but here it is in all things. I have the capacity. There is heaven in what you know and in what I know right here on earth. I can see it. You can, too. Heaven is pure happiness. Why not derive that happiness from all things that exist? It would be a waste not to. It may come, if you believe, at the end of your life on earth. It may also come, if you believe, during your life on earth. Belief is all that is necessary.

I sit here, looking out at the alley, and I know. I know I am glad to be here waiting for the trucks to show up. I know the drivers who come in are good guys and gals, and it is great to talk with them. It is wonderful to hear their stories. I know I have more to learn, myself; more stories yet to experience and then tell. I also know I have learned a few things so far and have a few to tell right now. I know because I have made mistakes and have realized why. I know I should have died several times. I know that without my family, I would probably be dead right now. It's a weird thing to tell your wife, but I tell her I would be dead without her. The reality is I would. I've survived but not without help, and I understand that. That help has come when I least expected it and from where I least expected. That help can only come when you realize that no possessions are necessary to completely enjoy each moment with the beautiful moon.

From the Abyss   John Emil Augustine

Love Seen From Hell

I emailed Kim one day in April 2005. The weather was warming. The walk to my truck from Jake's house each morning became easier. I struggled less against the cold wind as I got the door unlocked. Little rivers flowed down the alley, cutting the four-inch layer of ice in several parallel but crooked trickling slices.

Kim invited me over so I went. Her new apartment was nice. We sat on the couch and watched a movie that I didn't want to watch. I wanted to talk about everything that had happened between us. After the movie, I broached the subject.

"Kim, can we talk?"

"Sure. We're talking."

"I mean about what happened."

"What do you mean?"

"I want to tell you I'm sorry."

"Ok. Good."

"Are you ok?"

"I'm fine."

This wasn't going so well.

"I mean…I was an ass."

"I don't want to talk about that."

"I think we have to."

"I don't want to."

"Ok."

"Let's just start from here."

"Ok. I just think…"

"John, just stop. I'm not talking about that."

Thus began our new routine. Every other night I went to her place, and we would cook and watch TV or walk to a restaurant. The walks in the spring air were nice. Kim was beautiful as always. I loved to watch her walk. She was up-beat and happy. I thought maybe we would settle into each other, and everything would come full-circle. It seemed like a symmetrical ending to the four-year episode. Near the end of my time living with Jake and his wife, we all went out for sushi one night. They loved Kim. How could they not? She was pure joy.

But alone, in her apartment, the subject of our past hung over me. I needed to say my piece. I needed her to tell me her feelings. But every time I would bring it up, she deflected. When I slept over, she would move far to her side of the bed, and we would sleep. Our kisses were always quick and halted. I had run into indifference.

One night she said, "Let's be a couple."

"What?"

"Us. Kim and John. A couple."

"I don't get it."

"That's what you want, isn't it?"

"Well, yes."

"Ok. Then it's settled."

Only nothing really changed. It was a strange, cold shoulder that I looked at from the left side of the bed. It was elected indifference. We did couple-like activities, but never had intimate couple-like moments: never talked, never really kissed, were never close in any way.

I began inviting myself over less often, wondering if that would make a difference. Wondering if Kim would notice. Perhaps she did, but she never mentioned it. Soon I was down to once visit per week. Then once every-other week. It didn't seem to matter. She wouldn't talk about it. None of it seemed to matter to her.

It was an odd place to be. We were a couple, according to her. But it didn't matter where I was or what I did. If I were there, that was ok. If I were gone, that was ok, too. She didn't not want me around, but she didn't necessarily want me around. It seemed as simple as that.

All this time, I had wanted this. I got to be Kim's boyfriend again. But what had mattered to me didn't seem to matter to her. She was still beautiful. Her curly blonde hair still cascaded in little springs around her gorgeous face. Her smile still was wonderful to look at. Her voice still sounded like sweet, beautiful music. But none of it existed for me. None of it enveloped my being. I had returned to paradise and found it paved over. What was once heaven was now an indifferent purgatory.

From the Abyss   John Emil Augustine

I returned time and again to that former paradise, now more of a parking lot, looking for signs that it had been moved, remade, or otherwise existed in a new state, but all I knew was what I saw. You return to your childhood house which you have seen so often in pictures to find the trees grown, the landscape changed, the paint altered, the deck removed, the neighborhood run down, the distance between houses shorter – everything different than before. One day maybe you return to find it gone – the neighborhood re-zoned and now a freeway.

So you drive right over the spot where you spent your entire childhood, traveling at 65 mph. And that spot exists in a completely different, anonymous reality. If one is famous, he or she may get a sign marking the space. The sign is sped past. Few see it. Fewer stop. Fewer yet know its significance. And that's if you're famous. Everybody else gets nothing: no sign, no story.

Perhaps the story behind the sign, especially if it marks what had been a paradise, could inspire a new paradise. Perhaps. If it were read and understood. Perhaps if the sign were explained effectively enough, it would mean something to those who would otherwise have missed it. Perhaps the sign could even warn someone or teach something.

But most people whiz by at 65 or 70 mph, missing such signs. Missing such stories. We all miss most of them. You can't stop and read everything. Most of the time you have to smack head-on into a sign before you actually see it. Then perhaps, having seen it, you will read it. That is, if it isn't written in Martian. Martian can be so hard to understand.

One week Kim was sick, and I begged her to let me bring her soup or bath salts. I pleaded with her over texts and email, "Please let me bring you something to make you feel better." I called on the phone and left a message saying I would be there whenever she needed. She never returned my call. And I mean she literally never called. Ever again.

Paradise gone, I left its graveyard. Time had altered it. I had altered it. I had found it for an instant, and in another instant, had found it gone. But while paradise was missing, I was not. I was still around to know about it. I was still there to tell about it, maybe to post some kind of sign about it.

From the Abyss John Emil Augustine

But what had there been worth posting about? Would a non-existent paradise really be worth mentioning? Was there some lesson to be learned? What had paradise taught me while I was immersed in it? And why me? Why not someone more deserving with better decision-making skills and an easier story to tell? Why had I fallen into paradise, then been forced to leave, and then been allowed to see it completely altered beyond recognition? These questions would weigh on me for years. Still do.

I simply stopped calling Kim. The phone rings both ways. It never rang my way, when I was with her and when I was without her. I was making the relationship, not her. I was simply standing in the vacant parking lot, imagining what had been.

I knew I *had* been there. I *had* experienced it. I knew I had because I still felt the salve the paradise had given me. In that time, I had learned the difference between a relationship in which you both put one person first and a relationship in which both put the other person first. Before I'd met Kim, I had never been put first. Being in that position was paradise to me. Because of her, I learned I could receive that kind of love. I learned I didn't have to do the relationship all by myself.

But once the lesson was learned, the place in which I had learned it disappeared. Kim was no longer what she had been. She had taught me all this and then left. Yes, I could still call, still visit the thing that was once her, but it wasn't the same anymore. It was as if an angel had appeared by the campfire, coaxed me over, and gave me exactly what I needed: love. That was Kim. She was an angel, at least for that brief moment. Having displayed a bit of what heaven could be on earth, just long enough that I would catch on, the angel had gone. Kim herself remained in her sweet state, but the part of her that had shown me that wonderful paradise, the angel, was no longer visible.

Was it a trick of the mind? Maybe. Maybe I was in a place to believe there was a figurative heaven because the contrast was so blatant as viewed from my figurative hell. But were the heaven and hell figurative or real? Maybe it's the difference between simile and metaphor. Was I shown something *like*, or was I *actually* shown heaven?

Had Kim never appeared, I would never have known the contrast between heaven and hell; simile, metaphor, or otherwise. I had, of course, heard of heaven and hell, but they were only concepts to me before these events. They were cliché concepts at that. I no longer look at them as cliché, however, because I have experienced them. How we look at a thing makes its very essence appear differently depending on our vantage point.

Was the paradise a trick of mind? Perhaps, but no more than any other trick of mind that exists as a puzzle piece making up a minutia of this existence. If the place from which you stand can make an object look different, the situation in which you stand can make another situation look different as well. Was Kim truly an angel, at least for that brief time? Had she shown me a true paradise in which love heals and doesn't manipulate or constantly put itself first? From my vantage today, I have no doubt of either. You can say it was like or you can say it actually was. The difference is so negligible, it does not even exist to me.

I still don't know why an angel came and helped me, but I know one did. I don't know why I was healed, but I know I was. I also don't know why the angel didn't stay, but I know she didn't. I do know I began to look for relationships that were like the one I had been shown. I know I finally understood the Martian writing on the sign and finally knew which way to turn; I knew what to look for and what I was looking at. I finally learned that giving love and accepting love can never be mutually exclusive. Perhaps I needed help learning all this so I would be in a position to receive the gift of love from my current wife. Perhaps I was led to her and perhaps someone or some angel is still looking out for me and aiding me in some way. Or maybe I'm learning all this on my own.

But I doubt it. I couldn't do a relationship on my own, so I doubt I could learn such things about a relationship on my own either. I know, as a guy, it makes sense to me to be able to do everything on my own. It made so much sense that the signs saying otherwise were alien. But from my new vantage point, the vantage point I now have, the alien writing was nothing more than common sense written in perfect English. An angel was nothing more than the personification of love. And heaven was nothing more than love seen from hell.

Perhaps my new viewpoint helped in preparing me for what was to come. I certainly needed every bit of wisdom I could get for all that was about to happen to me, though of course I only know this in retrospect. Now, having given up on the notion of Kim and me, I stood at the bottom of an emotional void trying to find the sign pointing the way out.

After all, I had gone through all this but had not yet had the time to develop any perspective. From my viewpoint, I had just gotten my butt kicked, and that was all I knew. But endings are always beginnings. How I got from there to here and how I developed the perspective I currently have is its own story.

My journey was only beginning.

Coming Soon from John Emil Augustine:

From the Abyss II

~ Chapter One Excerpt ~

Lindbergh Field

My plane touched down in San Diego, and I immediately texted two words once my phone rebooted: "Just landed." It was a Thursday evening in May, 2005. The captain thanked us for flying as the plane taxied across the sunny pavement. The scene from my window a few minutes before had been beautiful as we made the final turn onto the runway below. The city sitting on the edge of the ocean looked a lot like Minneapolis, though Minneapolis was a river town. But the size of San Diego's downtown, and the sparse reflective skyscrapers reminded me of my own city. Only the extra presence of the ocean, blue and sparkling through my tiny airplane window, reminded me that I was not in Minneapolis.

What was I doing? I hadn't been on an airplane since I was a kid. I didn't travel. People with established lives traveled. Business people like the ones in the cheap suits surrounding me, the uniform of self-proclaimed importance, traveled to places like San Diego. I did not. This was not me at all. No one even knew I was doing this. My family didn't know I was gone. My ex-wife and my son knew nothing of my trip. Only my buddy Roland, whose house I was living in while he waited for the new occupants to take possession, knew of my trip. I was otherwise homeless, and he wanted his house to be occupied, so it was a mutually helpful arrangement. Except that I would be away for five days. So I had to let him know I would be gone. He was the only one who knew anything of my trip.

I sat in my seat watching everyone scramble for their carry-ons in the overhead compartments. Mine was up there, my only bag, but I wasn't in a hurry to get to a rental car or go find a second suitcase in the baggage claim. I didn't need either. So I just waited. A reply to my text came back: "I am here."

"Still on plane," I replied.

This was crazy. Like something out of a terrible movie with a plot I abhorred. One minute, I had been tallying the final grades for my last class of the semester, the next I was sitting on a plane in San Diego texting someone I had never seen in person. Was I insane? Stupid? Completely gullible? What ridiculous turn of events had put me here? Like a fading dream, I almost couldn't remember. I should have learned my lesson by now, by age thirty. I should have been wise to the trickery I was perhaps subjecting myself to. Why wasn't I smarter than this?

~Stay connected at johnemilaugustine.com~

- Get updates on John's next book and upcoming events
- Sign up for the newsletter and become part of the John Emil August-TEAM
- Follow John on his blog, Facebook, Twitter, Pinterest, and more
- Purchase official John Emil Augustine merchandise
- Invite John to be a speaker for your group or event
- Learn about other Master Koda authors and happenings
- Stay tuned for new surprises from John Emil Augustine

~ **Message from the Author** ~

Dear Reader,

As you have read, topics that fall under the umbrella of abuse or bullying are near and dear to me. My hope is to spread the message to those who are being abused, to those who know someone who is being abused, and to those who are abusing that we are here to help and respect each other, we are here to survive each other's abuse, and we are here to learn about and improve ourselves.

I believe abuse is in our nature. We take advantage of each other because we are animals. I don't mean that in a derogatory way. What I mean is when we study our own biology and cognition, we find we are animals in more ways than most of us care to recognize. But we are also human, and I believe being human means we are the ones in the animal kingdom who are most capable of learning, growing, and changing our behavior for the better.

There are times during which we want to remain ignorant of abuse. It is in our nature to wish for things to stay as they are. But in order to survive abuse, we must become aware; we must learn about ourselves, grow, and change for the better. Speaking up, or listening when someone else speaks up, is the first and most important part of helping and respecting each other. And it's often the hardest part.

What I hope to accomplish with this book series is to give readers the idea that abuse or "bullying" is all around us, and it is a part of life. Still, it's being part of life does not mean it has to continue. My story, sad as it is, I believe is still one of hope; of standing up from within despair and grabbing hold of the hand which is held out to you. Help and hope will come. Watch for them and in the meantime, protect yourself and those you know.

John Emil Augustine

P.S. If you enjoyed reading *From the Abyss Part I*, please consider reviewing it on Amazon.com. Your review will help get our message out there to those who need it. Thank you.

From the Abyss   John Emil Augustine